AN ORDINARY MIRACLE:
JOHN A. MACDONALD

An Ordinary Miracle: John A. Macdonald

Terry Julian, B.A., B.Ed., M.A.

Order this book online at www.trafford.com
or email orders@trafford.com

Most Trafford titles are also available at major online book retailers.

Layout and design by the Vancouver Desktop Publishing Centre
Published by Signature Publishing in conjuction with Trafford Publishing

Printed in Victoria, BC, Canada.

ISBN: 978-1-4269-1584-0 (sc)

*Our mission is to efficiently provide the world's finest, most comprehensive book publishing
service, enabling every author to experience success. To find out how to publish your book, your
way, and have it available worldwide, visit us online at www.trafford.com*

Trafford rev. 12/15/2009

 www.trafford.com

North America & international
toll-free: 1 888 232 4444 (USA & Canada)
phone: 250 383 6864 ♦ fax: 812 355 4082

To all Canadians

OTHER BOOKS BY TERRY JULIAN

The Candid Commission (1990)
Book Collecting for Everyone (1992)
A Capital Controversy (1994)
A British Lion (1998)
Be Amusing (2000)
Improving Canada's Democracy (2002)
Lions in Our Lives (2004)
Constantine, Christianity and Constantinople (2006)
The Seduction of Surveys in Canada's Federal Elections (2008)
An Ordinary Miracle: John A. Macdonald (2010)

List of Illustrations

(All photographs are by the author except where noted otherwise.)

Fathers of Confederation at the Quebec Conference in 1864. John A. Macdonald standing in the centre.

CHAPTER ONE

Introduction

"Let us be English or let us be French—but above all
let us be Canadians."

—*John A. Macdonald*

Rarely, throughout human history, circumstances unite which produce ordinary men and women of wisdom, talent, energy, and vision who create significant miracles.

Fortunately for Canada, John A. Macdonald was one of these ordinary persons and the miracle of Canada was the result.

His miraculous political accomplishments were achieved in spite of childhood difficulties, domestic problems, financial faults, drink failings, health infirmities, and no university education.

He achieved forty-six years, seven months and eleven days of federal political experience. He won eleven federal elections and was prime minister of Canada for nineteen years, making him the second longest serving P.M. of Canada. He is the only Canadian prime minister to win six majority governments.

Our political colossus is the Canadian equivalent of George Washington, the American, "father of his country."

This book has the task of illuminating John A. Macdonald as the father of Canada but also of explaining the man. These two parameters are dependent upon material which is a challenge of interpretation and selection. Some degree of selectivity is evident in any writing of history.

Fortunately, more has been written about him than any other person in Canadian biography. There are numerous books by eminent historians, a multitude of letters he wrote, and a considerable number of recorded speeches he made at meetings and in the House of Commons.

However, in spite of this, few Canadians know less significant details of his life. For example: that Sir John and Lady Macdonald visited New Westminster and Victoria in 1886; that in 1888 Charles Card, who was wanted for polygamy in the United States, went with two others to Prime Minister Macdonald asking for special dispensation to bring their plural wives and other families to Canada. Macdonald said no and the next year brought in legislation outlawing polygamy; that Macdonald was responsible for creating Canada's first national park—Banff, Alberta.

The mountain of literature on him has given most Canadians knowledge of the momentous achievement of Confederation in 1867, his vision and completion of Canada from sea to sea to sea and his initiative in building the transcontinental railway. He is, undoubtedly, the most illustrious miracle figure in the story of Canada but was an ordinary person with serious imperfections.

The most authoritative biography on Macdonald is Donald Creighton's two volume account published in 1952. This 1154 page work is entitled *John A. Macdonald, the Young Politician and the Old Chieftain.*

Creighton states Macdonald was among the early advocates of Canadian Confederation. In 1861 Macdonald made the following statement:

> *The government will not relax its exertions to effect a Confederation of the North American Provinces. We must however endeavour to take warning by the defects in the Constitution of the United States, which are now so painfully made manifest, and to form (if we succeed in a Federation) an efficient, central government.*[1]

Joseph Pope was Macdonald's secretary for the last ten years of our first Prime Minister's life. Pope's book, *Memoirs of the Right Honourable Sir John Alexander Macdonald*, contains a very complete

---

1   Richard Gwyn, John A., *The Man Who Made Us, 1815-1867*, page 228.

collection of private and public correspondence—hundreds of short and long letters that were dictated to him by Sir John.

As each new generation examines the material on Macdonald, more interpretations are written. Today, new books shed further light on this miraculous person.

In 2007, Richard Gwyn wrote an outstanding biography, entitled *John A., The Man Who Made Us 1815–1867*. It was the first volume that will eventually be a two volume series. This writer believes "the man who made us" is the best description of our first prime minister.

That same year also saw a Ray MacSkimming historical fiction book dealing with the year 1891 when John A. fought his final election battle. It depicts Macdonald as a kindly person.

Another book published in 2006 is Patricia Phenix's *Private Demons—the Tragic Personal Life of John A. Macdonald*. The emphasis is on John A.'s myriad problems and paints a very bleak picture. It does illustrate how remarkable he was to accomplish so much in spite of vicissitudes in his personal and political life.

All these books add to the concept of John A. being an ordinary miracle.

J. K. Johnson wrote in 1968, "Macdonald the man, especially the public man, has been more thoroughly examined, exposed and explained, than any other Canadian historical figure".[2]

The number of biographies and other material show that we should accept that John Macdonald's life, as in our own lives, is not absolutely white or absolutely black.

This book is written to focus on yet another view of Sir John A. Macdonald. It will convey, the author hopes, a sense of him as a living man, as a troubled person who was also a builder of dreams. And, personally, the author wishes Canadian citizens would take a renewed interest in his life and work, particularly the legacy of Confederation. Included are chapters on his personal and political life and the many legacies he left to Canadians, emphasizing, of course, the most important, that of Confederation.

---

2   J. K. Johnson, *Letters of John A. Macdonald*, Vol. 1, page 14.

The title could have been, "Following in the Footsteps of Sir John A. Macdonald," because the author visited many places associated with him, including the following:

In the city of Kingston there are numerous buildings where he spent his early career. There is his first law office where he began the practice of law in 1835. His second office in 1849 to 1860 and a third from 1860 to his death. He maintained a law practice throughout his political career. In the City Hall is the room where he attended meetings as a city alderman.

Ottawa has two lovely homes, "Stadacona" in Sandy Hill in which Sir John and Lady Macdonald stayed from 1878 to 1883 and "Earnscliffe" where he lived from 1883 to 1891 when he died. Unfortunately, both these mansions were sold to other countries.

The East Block of the Parliament Buildings has Sir John's restored office and the Privy Council Room and both are open to the public.

The Cataraqui Cemetery outside Kingston where he, his mother, his father, his first wife, his infant son and two sisters are buried.

We need an increased awareness of the influence of Sir John A. Macdonald on our lives. As J. L. Granatstein states, *"We have our history to restore. It matters less who tried to kill it then that we seize the opportunity to bring Canadian history back to life. It's a great story and a proud saga of nationhood. I believe Canada's history can inspire us all, those born here and those who choose to join us."*[3]

One final thought in this introduction. John A's life has undoubtedly a profound significance for Canadians. But the historical Macdonald is an interpretation because the materials we rely on—letters, speeches, ephemera, recollections—were examined and evaluated by authors and historians through their own senses and philosophy. Therefore, a fixed and complete portrait of him or any other historical figure is impossible. Each biographer, including this one, depends on his or her inferences, sense of importance and prejudices.

This is true of any historical explanation because no one can ever have complete evidence from the past.

---

3   J. L. Granatstein, *Who Killed Canadian History?* page 188.

The book title incorporates the words "ordinary miracle." This is taken from a verse of a song written by the Russian composer G. Gladkov in 1978.

When you wake up everyday
Please don't throw your dreams away
Hold them close to your heart
Cause we are all a part
Of the ordinary miracle

CHAPTER TWO

John A. Macdonald's Personal Life

> "Be to our faults a little blind, and to our virtues always kind."
>
> *—His favourite motto*

John Alexander Macdonald was born in Glasgow, Scotland, in 1815. The year 1815 is significant because the Battle of Waterloo was fought in that year and the Treaty of Ghent which officially ended the War of 1812 was signed in 1815.

The family emigrated to Kingston, Ontario, in 1820. It took the Macdonald family forty-two days to get from Glasgow to Quebec and twelve more to travel to Kingston. In 1820 Kingston had only 4000 citizens but was geographically important being located at the eastern end of Lake Ontario and the outlet of the St. Lawrence River.

Father Hugh opened a shop with the family living over it. The business was not financially successful. Later a grist mill was purchased outside of town on the Bay of Quinto which was equally unprofitable. The mill and house building are still standing today. The Macdonalds stayed there for five years.

When John was seven years of age he witnessed the killing of his five-year-old younger brother by a drunken child minder.

At age fifteen he left formal schooling and joined a law firm in Kingston as an apprentice. "I had no boyhood," he complained many years later. "From the age of sixteen, I began to earn my own living."[4]

---

4   Joseph Pope, *Memoirs of the Right Honourable Sir John Alexander Macdonald.* page 6.

Martello Tower, Kingston.

Kingston was of strategic importance as the southern terminus of the Rideau Canal which was built between 1826 and 1832. Fort Henry was rebuilt to protect it and in 1848 four Martello towers with guns were constructed at Kingston. These were constant reminders to Macdonald of the threat of the United States.

During his apprenticeship he lived at Rideau Street in Kingston and was admitted to the bar when he was twenty-one.

Although lacking higher education, he later acquired a vast fund of knowledge by reading.

In 1837 he was elected to the board of directors of the Commercial Bank and shortly after became the bank's solicitor.

John Macdonald was also a member of the militia which was called out in 1837 and 1838 to defend Upper Canada from border skirmishes by "patriots" and Americans. This also affected his thinking and led to his resistance to any attempt to weaken the union with Britain. The attacks resulted in the Durham Report which united Upper and Lower Canada into one government.

Kingston's Rideau Street house where Macdonald lived in his youth.

Rumors that Kingston would become the place of government for Upper and Lower Canada attracted new people and Macdonald became part of an ensuing building boom as he purchased a town lot on Brock Street and had a house built. It does not exist today.

Indeed, Kingston did become the capital of the newly united provinces of Upper and Lower Canada in 1841. The large, grand City Hall was erected in 1844 as part of its stature as a capital city. Unfortunately for Kingston, the capital was moved to Montreal that same year because of roars of disapproval from larger cities like Montreal and Toronto.

Today, the City Hall still stands, grandly overlooking the waterfront.

Macdonald's father did not live long enough to come to the Brock Street house as Hugh Macdonald died in 1841 at the age of fifty-four. However, his mother and two sisters moved there. So at twenty-six years of age, John Macdonald's mother and two middle age sisters became his total responsibility.

Kingston Town Hall.

He was frequently concerned about his health. His friends and associates said that at times he suffered from many colds, gallstones, bronchitis, sciatica, and cholera. His opponents suggested these were really over indulgence in drink and they were sometimes correct.

Excessive drinking was believed to have been a legacy from his father. In times of extreme stress or worry it engulfed him but did not interfere with his ability as a politician or as a husband. This is indeed miraculous.

This author believes that evidence indicates Macdonald's consumption of alcohol was greatly exaggerated. No one who drank as much as he was supposed to imbibe could have accomplished as much as he did. It feeds into the cynicism that so many citizens have about their politicians. This smug, hypocritical attitude towards political leaders adds to the myth that John A. Macdonald was a drunkard.

It should also be mentioned that men in general and most politicians

First Law Office.

drank a lot in the Victorian period. Whiskey was as low as twenty-five cents a gallon and in many homes a pail of whiskey was always available in the kitchen.

And, as we shall read later, John A. had domestic and political problems which sometimes led to long and troubled days leading to bottled relief. This was the shadow side of his personality.

However, he never made an attempt to hide his drinking and sometimes even referred to it as the following anecdotes show:[5]

At one time complaints were pretty numerous among prominent Conservative members of the drinking habits of Thomas D'Arcy McGee. A member came to John A. and said, 'You must speak to

---

5   E.B. Bigger. *Anecdotal Life of Sir John A. Macdonald*, pages 193-195.

Second Law Office.

him. This sort of thing is a disgrace.' After putting them off for some time, John A. went to McGee and said, 'Look here, McGee, this Government can't afford two drunkards, and you've got to stop.'

Sir John's very weakness was a secret of his popularity with a certain class of men and he did not hesitate to take advantage of the weakness when the occasion served his purpose. Once he caused great applause in his audience when he said, 'I know enough of the feeling of this meeting to know that you would rather have John A. drunk than George Brown sober.'

He had a health problem in 1842 and when doctors prescribed rest he went to England. While there he visited his cousin Isabella Clark. The next year she sailed to Canada to visit relatives in Kingston. Within months of her arrival, John A. and Isabella were married. She was thirty-four and he was twenty-eight. John took her to his home on Brock Street that he still shared with his mother and sisters.

Shortly after, Isabella developed a debilitating illness that lasted for the remainder of her life. Unable to determine the cause and helpless to cure it, doctors administered opium to relieve her pain. By 1845 she was taking opium in larger and larger doses but, in spite of this, delivered a baby boy who died before he was one year of age.

In 1850 another son was born named Hugh. This child was raised by John A.'s sisters.

Macdonald's thirteen sad years with Isabella came to an end with her death in 1857, aged forty-eight. Because she could not help her husband socially, John A. often referred to her as his "invisible lady."

John Creighton, Macdonald's most thorough biographer, attributes John A.'s increased drinking habits to bearing the cross of Isabella's illness and subsequent opium addiction.

Macdonald was in London in 1866 to help monitor Canada's new constitution through the British Parliament. He had drafted most of it in preparation for the Charlottetown and Quebec Conferences held earlier.

While in London, after nine years as a widower, John A. became engaged to Susan Agnes (Susy) Bernard, a lady he had met in Canada. They were married in London the next year. Macdonald was now fifty-two years old and Susan was his junior by twenty-two years.

That same year (1867) Confederation was proclaimed and Macdonald not only became the first Prime Minister of Canada but was knighted by Queen Victoria and was now Sir John A. Macdonald.

The couple returned to Ottawa and leased a row house called the "Quadrilateral." Ottawa at that time was a lumber town of about 20,000 people. No trace of the "Quadrilateral" exists today and the property at Daly Avenue and Cumberland Street does not even have a plaque marking the site.

Following the exciting days of the celebration of Confederation on July 1, 1867 and the early days of marriage, Sir John's financial problems emerged. His debt to the failed Commercial Bank at Kingston was $80,000 because he was a director. As Prime Minister

Site of Macdonald's Quadrilateral House in Ottawa.

he had only a salary of $5000. In addition he obtained $1700 a year from his Kingston law office. It took years to pay off his debts.

In 1868, on April 7, Macdonald was notified late that night that his friend and colleague Thomas D'Arcy McGee was murdered by an Irish union supporter. Sir John rushed to his friend's lodging and helped move the body inside.

The next afternoon Prime Minister Macdonald gave a tribute to McGee in the House of Commons.

Mister Speaker, it was with pain amounting to anguish that I rise to address you. He who last night was with us and of us, whose voice is still ringing in our ears, who charmed us with his marvellous eloquence, elevated us by his large statesmanship, and instructed us by his wisdom and his patriotism, is no more, is foully murdered. If ever a soldier who fell on the field of battle in the front of the fight, deserved well of his country, Thomas D'Arcy McGee deserved well of Canada and its people. The blow which has just fallen is too recent, the shock is too great, for us to yet realize its awful atrocity, or the extent of this most irreparable loss. I feel, sir, that our sorrow, genuine and unaffected sorrow, prevents us from giving adequate expression to our feelings just now, but by and by, and at length, the House will have a melancholy pleasure in considering the character and position of my late friend and colleague. To all, the loss is great, to me I may say inexpressibly so; as the loss is not only of a warm political friend, who has acted with me for some years, but of one with whom I enjoyed the intercommunication of his rich and varied mind; the blow has been overwhelming. I feel altogether incapable of addressing myself to the subject just now. Our departed friend was a man of the kindest and most generous impulse, a man whose hand was open to every one, whose heart was made for friendship, and whose enmities were written in water; a man who had no gall and no guile.

He might have lived a long and respected life had he chosen the easy path of popularity rather than the stern one of duty. He has lived a short life, respected and beloved, and died a heroic death; a martyr to the cause of his country. How easy it would have been for him, had he chosen, to have sailed along the full tide of popularity with thousands and hundreds of thousands following him, without the loss of a single plaudit, but has been slain, and I fear slain because he preferred the path of duty.

He has gone from us, and it will be long ere we find such a happy mixture of eloquence and wisdom, wit and earnestness. His was of no artificial or meretricious eloquence, every word of his was as he believed, and every belief, every thought of his, was in the direction of what was good and true.[6]

1869 brought another tragedy when the birth of a daughter Mary occurred. She was born with hydrocephalus, an incurable birth defect, and suffered from physical and mental difficulties. She was never able to take care of herself and was still a cripple when she died in 1933 at sixty-four years of age.

What Mary's condition cost Agnes and Sir John no one can know but both were devoted to her. Macdonald read to Mary for hours

---

6   Brian Busby, *Great Canadian Speeches*, page 176.

from children's books. He was the only person who called her his "Baboo," a term of endearment.

One summer Mary was away from home with her grandmother and Sir John wrote the following letter to her:[7]

My dearest Mary,

You must know that your kind Mama and I are very anxious to see you and Granny again. We have just put a new carpet in your room and got everything ready for you.

The garden looks lovely just now. It is full of beautiful flowers and I hope you will see them before they are withered.

There are some fine melons in the garden. You must pick them for dinner and feed the chickens with the rind. You remember that Mama cut my hair and made me look like a crippled donkey. It was grown quite long again. When you come home you must not pull it too hard.

I intend to have some new stories for you when you come in the morning into Papa's bed and cuddle him up.

Give my love to dear good Grand Mamma and give her a kiss for me . . . and so goodbye my pet and come home soon to your loving papa.

John A.

In 1871 the Macdonalds rented "Earnscliffe" during the winter and then moved back to the "Quadrilateral."

From 1878 to 1883 they lived in the stately "Stadacona Hall." (Stadacona was the Indian name for Quebec and was located in the Sands Hills area, reasonably close to Parliament Hill.) The house had been built in 1871 for a lumber merchant named John Cameron. It was sold in the 1990s to the Government of Brunei. It is on Laurier Avenue just a few doors from Laurier House which was later the home of Sir Wilfred Laurier and Mackenzie King and is now owned by Canada and open to the public.

---

7   Ainslie Manson, *Baboo, The Story of Sir John A. Macdonald's Daughter,* page 11.

Sir John bought the house called by him, Earnscliffe (Eagles Cliff) in 1883 for $10,000 and lived in it until his death in 1891. More on this historic home in Chapter Seven.

The Macdonalds had no more children after Mary and neither of his two surviving offspring had heirs.

After a bitter election campaign victory in 1872, Sir John collapsed with an attack of gallstones. After his recovery he began more drinking. The Pacific Railway scandal in 1873 caused him to resign but he returned to power in 1878, 1887 and 1891.

In 1885 the transcontinental railway was completed to the coast of British Columbia. Sir John and Lady Macdonald took the train from Ottawa to Port Moody in 1886 with stops along the way. One of them was Banff Alberta which Macdonald had designated as the first national park in 1885.

A side trip from Port Moody to New Westminster was arranged and was reported in that city's newspaper on August 18, 1886.

Sir John A. MacDonald was entertained in a room in the old Government House at Sapperton—an antechamber of the old ballroom. After lunch, the mayor of New Westminster (Dickinson) read the address prepared by the Council, mentioned the great railway and its branch line and hoped for improved navigation on the Fraser River.

Mayor McLean of Vancouver next appeared on the platform and thanked the mayor of New Westminster for the noble efforts he made to assist the sufferers of the fire at Vancouver.[8]

After the reception at Government House, Macdonald enjoyed a tour of New Westminster's Columbia Street in a horse drawn cart.

The Macdonalds next stop was the capital Victoria which he had represented as M.P. from 1878 to 1882.

The capital was moved from New Westminster to Victoria in 1868 and of the Government House in Sapperton, New Westminster, nothing remains.

---

8 Alan Woodland, *Eminent Guests*, City of New Westminster, page 41.

As the reader will read in the next chapter, Sir John showed a high intelligence mixed with generosity, tolerance, resilience, patience and shrewd political common senses. Sometimes the patience aspect of his personality became procrastination as the following indicates:

It is perhaps significant that during Macdonald's lifetime many believed that his nickname 'Old Tomorrow' was given him by a western Indian chief—either Poundmaker or Crowfoot . . . Indian chiefs had good reason to resent Macdonald's habit of putting problems off until tomorrow . . . Macdonald knew about his nickname. When it was rumoured that he was to be elevated to a British peerage, he was asked what title he would take. With a perfectly straight face he replied: 'Lord Tomorrow.'[9]

His sense of humour was part of his personality.

On one occasion Governor General Lord Dufferin delivered an address in Greek before the University of McGill College, Sir John Macdonald and Sir Hector Langevin being present with him. One of the reporters wrote in his report: 'His Lordship spoke in the purest ancient Greek without mispronouncing a word or making the slightest grammatical solecism.'
'Good Heavens,' said Sir Hector to Sir John, as they read the report. 'How did the reporter know that?'
'I told him,' replied Sir John.
'But you don't know Greek.'
'True,' answered Sir John, 'but I know a little about politics.'[10]

When he visited Prince Edward Island in 1890, he was asked to sign the visitors' book in the legislative library. He listed his occupation as "cabinet-maker."

---

9 Donald Swainson, *John A. Macdonald: The Man and the Politician*, page 130.
10 E. B. Biggar, *Anecdotal Life of Sir John Macdonald*, page 223.

He also had a personal magnetism which attracted people to him. And, important too, was his uncanny memory for names of persons and the family history connected to them. Although he was not bilingual he was greatly respected by the majority of his French speaking friends.

Another aspect of Macdonald's personality is revealed by Joseph Pope in his "Memoirs."

The following incident, related to me by the Baroness Macdonald of Earnscliffe, affords a good illustration of the affectionate nature of my old chief. More than thirty years after the time of which I am now writing, Lady Macdonald was looking over some odds and ends at Earnscliffe, when she came upon a box of child's toys—a broken rattle, a small cart, and some animals, etc. Not knowing to whom they belonged, she took them to Sir John, who was lying on his bed. He looked at them at first carelessly, then thoughtfully, raised himself on his elbow, and took one up in his hand. 'Ah!' said he, 'those were little John A.'s.' He had kept beside him these mementos of his little boy all those years. Lady Macdonald replaced the box almost reverently where she found it, and it is there to-day.[11]

Macdonald's political morality was often questioned but he did try to be careful in his relations with anyone who might ask a favour of him as an M.P. or Prime Minister as Pope relates:

One morning, in the month of January, a gentleman reputed very well off, called at Earnscliffe, and after transacting the business that had brought him there, said, "Sir John, I know you are having a hard time of it in Kingston. I know, too, you are not over-well provided with this world's goods. I should very much like to be allowed to give you a sub-scription towards defraying your own election expenses.' With that he put down an envelope containing a considerable sum of money, and took his leave before Sir John could say a word. I was not in the room at the time, but during the day Sir John told me of it, adding 'I know that—is actuated by the best of motives, and I would not hurt his feelings for the

---

[11] Pope, *Memoirs*, page 622.

world; nevertheless, in view of the fact that he is (or recently has been) a Government contractor, it would not do for me to touch a penny of this. I want you to take this package, seek out——, and return it to him with my thanks, explaining why it is impossible for me to accept his kind aid.' This I did on the same day.

Some years before the date of which I have been speaking, Sir John, during one summer, occupied the country house of a friend who had relations with the Government. At the end of the season he inquired as to the rent, and was informed there was nothing to pay. This he would not hear of. It was in vain that the owner represented that Sir John had done him a service by occupying a house that otherwise would have remained empty. He insisted upon paying full value for the use of the property, and, the owner remaining obdurate, he sent his cheque by post.[12]

Another domestic story again shows sensitivity to any impropriety.

When the city of Vancouver was in its infancy, or, rather, before there was any city there at all, lady Macdonald one day expressed the wish to purchase two lots on what is now the town site, and asked Sir John's permission to do so.

Said she, 'I don't want any money, I have three or four hundred dollars of my own, and the Colonel' (her brother) 'will give me three or four hundred more.'

'No, my dear,' he replied, 'you had better not!'

'Why?' said Lady Macdonald.

'Well, if you were to buy any lots out there, the first thing I should know would be that a post-office or a customhouse was put on them without my knowing anything about it, and I should have it thrown at me in Parliament that you had been paid for them ten cents more than they were worth.'

So the lots were never bought.[13]

---

12 *Ibid.*, page 253.
13 Granatstein, page 157.

Nothing reveals the humanity of Sir John more than a letter he wrote in the last year of his life to a little girl in Ontario.

She had written him for his seventy-sixth birthday to tell him that her birthday was on the same day as his . . . She [also] complained that a young fellow she had written to had never replied to her . . .

> *Earnscliffe, Ottawa*
> *January 6, 1891*
> *My dear little Friend,*
> *I am glad to get your letter to know that next Sunday you and I will be of the same age [!] I hope and believe however that you will see many more birthdays than I shall, and I trust that every birthday may find you strong in health, and prosperous, and happy.*
> *I think it was mean of that young fellow not to answer your letter—You see, I have been longer in the world than he, and know more than he does of what is due to young ladies.*
> *I send you a dollar note with which pray buy some small keepsake to remember me by, and*
> *Believe me,*
> *Yours sincerely,*
> *John A. Macdonald.*[14]

Of course, Sir John did not have another birthday and died in June, 1891.

Lena Newman[15] estimated that he wrote and signed over 30,000 pieces of correspondence and these often show that he really cared for those around him. He never neglected to write regularly to his mother and sister.

Today, there are many authors who compliment Macdonald. Tom Axworthy says of him:

No one was beneath him, and no one was ever forgotten. He knew

---

14 P. B. Waite, *Macdonald*, page 211.

15 Newman, Lena. *The John A. Macdonald Album*. Tundra Books, Montreal, Quebec, 1974, page 10.

kings and presidents, but on the mantle of his library, at Earnscliffe,
was a picture of Eliza Grimason, a tavern keeper from Kingston who
drove him in his early campaigns.[16]

Authoritative historian Donald Creighton wrote, "He knew
Canadians better than anybody had ever known them before—and
better than anyone would ever know them again."[17]

In 1998 Christopher Moore said, "Personal skills were where
Macdonald shone."[18]

Part of this was his phenomenal memory for names and faces.
Edwin Guillet illustrates this in his 1967 book.[19]

George Guillet, M.P. for West Northumberland in Sir John's day,
told me of the great impression the Chief made in his constituency
during a campaign of the eighties. 'I introduced him to twenty or
thirty farmers in a rural schoolhouse,' he said, 'and after chatting
with them for half an hour he called each one by name as he shook
hands before continuing on to the next meeting. Not one of these
farmers could ever do enough for Sir John thereafter, and they never
forgot that they had shaken hands with the Prime Minister.'

We now turn to Macdonald's political life and his genius in uniting the people of Canada within the same federation so that they
could work together for the common good and still maintain their
individual characteristics.

---

16 Tom Axworthy, in *The Hill Times*, July 21, 2008 edition.
17 Donald Creighton, *John A. Macdonald, the Young Politician and the Old
   Chieftain.* page 231.
18 Christopher Moore, page 205.
19 Edwin Guillet, *You'll Never Die John A.*, page 72.

CHAPTER THREE

John A. Macdonald's Political Life to Confederation

"Anyone may support me when I am right. What I want is a man that will support me when I am wrong."

—*John A. Macdonald*

John A. was introduced to politics in 1843 at the age of twenty-eight when he was elected as a city alderman in Kingston. He won with 156 votes over his opponent who had 93. As alderman he was an active supporter in establishing Queen's University at Kingston.

The next year (1844) he ran in the provincial election for the legislature of the province of Canada representing Kingston. His letter to the electors included a principle he held all his life—allegiance to Great Britain.

> *To the Free and Independent Electors of the Town of Kingston.*
> *Gentlemen,*
> *The approaching election calls upon me to redeem the pledge made in March last, in answer to the flattering requisition addressed to me by 225 electors, inviting me to become a candidate for the representation of this town.*
> *A residence in Kingston since infancy has afforded every opportunity to me of knowing the wants and claims of our 'Loyal Old Town,' and to you of ascertaining my political opinions, and my qualifications for the office I now solicit at your hands.*

I, therefore, need scarcely state my firm belief that the prosperity of Canada depends upon its permanent connection with the Mother Country, and that I shall resist to the utmost any attempt (from whatever quarter it may come) which may tend to weaken that union.

The proposed measures for reducing the enormous expense of the public departments, for improving the system of common schools, and for opening and extending the advantages of our Collegiate Institutes, will receive my cordial support.

It is alike my duty and my interest to promote the prosperity of this city and the adjacent country. No exertion will be spared by me in forwarding the settlement of our rear townships, by the formation of public roads, in assisting and concentrating the trade of this port, and in such other local measures as well in any way conduce [contributing] to your advantage.

I am deeply grateful for the confidence you have already reposed in me; and trusting that I have done nothing to forfeit it, I have the honour to be,

Your obliged and faithful servant,
John A. Macdonald[20]

He easily won that election and was appointed Receiver-General in 1847.

After a period of only ten months another election resulted in a government defeat in 1848.

The cause of the election was the "Rebellion Losses Bill," which provided indemnification of persons in Lower Canada whose property had been destroyed during the rebellion of 1837 and 1838.

Macdonald opposed the bill and denounced it as "a most shameful one."

The bill passed third reading and caused riots in Montreal in which the Parliament Buildings were burned. This resulted in the removal of the capital to Quebec and Toronto—changing every two years. This inconvenient arrangement lasted until Queen Victoria chose Ottawa as the permanent capital in 1865.

---

20 Cynthia Smith and Jack McLeod, *Sir John A.*, page 6.

Government house where the Charlottetown Conference was held.

After the 1848 defeat, Macdonald worked to build up the Conservative Party. In 1851 and again in 1854 he was re-elected as M.L.A. for Kingston and in the 1854 election he joined a coalition cabinet as Attorney General.

At this time Macdonald was able to gradually create a party which was made up of diversified groups; French and English, Orange Irish and Green Irish, Catholics and Anglicans and Methodists.

In 1857 he was again re-elected by 1189 votes to 7 in Kingston and became joint Prime Minister of the province of Canada with Etienne-Paschal Taché and later George Etienne Cartier.

In 1861 there was another election and Macdonald again won over his opponent 758 votes to 474. In St. Thomas, Ontario, he said,

I am like those who hear me, a Canadian heart and soul . . . That, I believe is the feeling that exists in every breast here; and though I have the misfortune . . . to be a Scotchman, still I caught young and was brought to this country before I was very much corrupted.

Charlottetown Conference Room (restored).

[Laughter] Since I was five years old, I have been in Canada. All my hopes and dreams and my remembrances are Canadian; not only are my principles and prejudices Canadian but what, as a Scotchman, I feel as much as anyone else, my interests are Canadian. [Applause][21]

In that year (1861) the American Civil War began.

From 1862 to 1864 there was a political deadlock between Canada East (Quebec) and Canada West (Ontario). In these three years, four cabinets resigned and there were two general elections. In all, four governments in three years.

This impasse was overcome in 1864 when George Brown, opposition Liberal leader, offered to support a government which would pursue a federal union of the provinces. Macdonald welcomed this arrangement because he had always been a fervent nationalist when many Canadians were localists or provincialists.

---

21 Richard Gwyn, *The Man Who Made Us*, page 298.

Charlottetown Conference delegates (Macdonald sitting, centre), 1864.

The "Great Coalition" government was a uniquely brilliant move that put an end to the frustrating situation which preceded it and provided a mechanism for attempting a Confederation of all the British colonies.

It heralded the Charlottetown Conference held from September 1 to 12, 1864, which ostensibly was to discuss Maritime Union but other delegates from Canada (Quebec and Ontario) including Macdonald were invited.

At that conference, Macdonald and Cartier gave general arguments in favour of a wider Confederation.

What they did was to show that a wider union was practical and that it could come to fruition by the twenty-three delegates seated in Government House, Charlottetown.

Macdonald moved a resolution, "that the best interests and the present and future prosperity of British North America will be promoted by a federal union under the Crown of Great Britain, provided such union can be effected on principles just to the several provinces."[22]

---

22 M. Hammond, *Confederation and Its Leaders*, page 29.

Quebec Conference building 1864.

In a Halifax speech immediately after the Charlottetown Confer-ence, Macdonald said in part, "The Confederation scheme reflected the ambition of men who would be big. For twenty long years I have been dragging myself through the dreary waste of colonial politics. I thought there was no end, nothing worthy of ambition, but now I see something which is well worthy of all that I have suffered."[23]

A month later a second Confederation Conference was held at Quebec City commencing October 10, 1864. At those meetings the delegates agreed to seventy-two resolutions giving the rules of gov-ernment. Macdonald had drafted fifty of these in just two weeks. They established the outline for a United Canada and would later be made into the British North America Act that established Confederation.

The task of framing the resolutions fell to Macdonald because there was little legal expertise among the twenty-three Fathers of Confederation. He later told a friend: "As it is I have no help. What-ever is good or ill in the Constitution is mine."[24]

23 M. Bliss, *Right Honourable Man*, page 16.
24 Peter Waite, *The Illustrated History of Canada*, page 326.

Quebec Conference delegates, Macdonald seated on the left, 1864.

What ideas did Macdonald want in the new Canada? He wanted a centralized federal system and had always favoured a strong central government. He stated these concepts to the delegates in Quebec and ended with these words:

> *Then we shall have a great step in advance of the American Republic. It can only attain that objective with rigorous general government—we shall not have New Brunswickers, nor Nova Scotians, nor Canadians, but British Americans under the sway of the British Sovereign . . . I hope that we will be enabled to work out a constitution that will have a strong central government, able to offer a powerful resistance to any force whatever, and at the same time will preserve for each Province its own identify, and will protect every ambition.*[25]

---

25 Hammond, page 7.

Painting of the Fathers of Confederation at Quebec in 1864, Macdonald standing in the centre.

After this brilliant and moving address, a motion was passed to favour the federal union. As part of the centralized federal system, Ottawa would appoint provincial lieutenant governors and senators. It would also control banking and money.

Immigration and agriculture would be joint jurisdictions. The federal government would assume all provincial debt and provide revenue for the provinces on the basis of population.

On the need for a Senate Macdonald was very clear.

Among constitutional questions few possess for Sir John Macdonald greater interest than the bicameral system . . . His view of the necessity for a second chamber may be expressed briefly by the story told of Washington, which Sir John was fond of relating. It is said that on his return from France, Jefferson called Washington to account for having agreed to a second chamber.

'Of what use is the Senate?' he said, as he stood before the fire with a cup of tea in his hand, pouring the tea into his saucer as he spoke.

'You have answered your own question,' replied Washington.

'What do you mean?'

'Why did you pour that tea into your saucer?'
'To cool it,' quoth Jefferson.
'Even so,' said Washington, 'the Senate is the saucer into which we
pour legislation to cool.'
This illustration, Sir John used to say, was perfect.[26]

After much discussion John A. moved that the Senate be composed of twenty-four members from each of Canada East, Canada West, and the four Atlantic provinces.

As has been mentioned, seventy-two resolutions on Confederation were debated and passed. How to amend the Constitution was not discussed.

It was at the Quebec Conference that the artist Robert Harris painted the official portrait of the Fathers of Confederation. Unfortunately, the painting was hung in the centre block of the parliament buildings which was destroyed in the fire of 1916. A sketch that Harris had made earlier was used to create a work that has been reproduced countless times. It is in many classrooms and hundreds of buildings throughout Canada. For example, in the Railway Committee Room of Parliament there is a large picture which hangs at the south end (see page 39).

It is also on china plates and other memorabilia, particularly in 1967 when Canada celebrated one hundred years of Confederation.

There were many suggestions on what to call the new "United Canada." Competing names included: the United Colony of Canada, the United Provinces of Canada, the Federated Provinces of Canada, the Republic of Canada, the Realm of Canada, the Union of Canada, the Kingdom of Canada, and the Dominion of Canada.

The Dominion of Canada was agreed to by the Fathers of Confederation. It had been suggested by the Premier of New Brunswick, Samuel Tilley, from Psalm 72, verse 8, "May he have dominion from sea to sea."[27]

---

26 Joseph Pope, *Memoirs*, Vol. 2, page 233.

27 Edward Hird, *Battle for the Soul of Canada*, page 133.

And so the two sunny weeks in Charlottetown and the three rainy ones in Quebec City produced concrete arrangements for a union.

This framework now went to the provinces for month-long debates. Fear of the possible annexation of Canada to the United States was a major force driving provincial leaders towards unity.

It is difficult to understand today that in the 1860's most people in Canada were fearful of the "Manifest Destiny" of the American republic to occupy the entire continent.

Several events during the American Civil War (1861-1865) influenced that anxiety. In 1861 there was the "Trent Affair" in which North soldiers arrested two Confederate diplomats who were going to England on the British ship "Trent." Britain sent troops to Canada, but tensions were relaxed when the prisoners were released.

There was also the "Chesapeake" incident in 1863 when the North captured a ship by that name in British territorial waters.

In 1864 Confederates robbed three Northern banks in Vermont and fled into Canada. Northern troops were ordered to pursue the robbers and kill them. Fortunately, President Lincoln revoked the order.

It was also in that same year that British Prime Minister Gladstone issued a memorandum arguing that no effort by Britain could defend the Canadian provinces against the overwhelming army of the United States.

This was the realization that at the end of the Civil War in the United States in 1865, the Grand Army of the Republic of 800,000 men was available to invade Canada and many northern U.S. newspapers suggested that it do so.

In debates on Confederation, Macdonald claimed that one of "the great advantages of Confederation is that we shall have a united concerted and uniform system of defence."[28]

Additionally, in 1865 and 1866, there were small invasions into Canada by Fenians (Irish Americans) who wished to hurt England in an attempt to free Ireland. The attacks failed but reinforced argu-

---

28 Ged Martin, *Britain and the Origins of Confederation*, page 63.

ments that Confederation was necessary for national security as many Canadians thought the United States had encouraged the raids.

Even on the far western coast of British Columbia there was, after the 1858 gold rush of American miners, the fear of a possible invasion from the South. This was why, as early as 1859, Colonel Moody with a contingent of Royal Engineers decided that the capital of British Columbia would not be at Fort Langley but on the west side of the Fraser River at New Westminster, which could be more easily defended.

After the provincial debates were complete in 1865, resolutions went to the House of Commons. At that time Macdonald said in part:

> . . . *We can now take advantage of the experience of the last seventy-eight years, during which their Constitution has existed, and I am strongly of the belief that we have, in a great measure, avoided in this system which we propose for the adoption of the people of Canada, the defects which time and events have shown to exist in the American Constitution . . . Ever since the union was formed the difficulty of what is called "State Rights" has existed, and this had much to do in bringing on the present unhappy war in the United States.*
>
> . . . *In conclusion, I would again implore the House not to let this opportunity to pass. It is an opportunity that may never recur. At the risk of repeating myself, I would say, it was only by a happy concurrence of circumstances, that we were enabled to bring this great question to its present position. If we do not take advantage of the time, if we show ourselves unequal to the occasion, it may never return, and we shall hereafter bitterly and unavailingly regret having failed to embrace the happy opportunity now offered of founding a great nation . . .*[29]

To further his view to remain connected to Great Britain, Macdonald wanted the Governor-General to be chosen by the Queen. (After Canada achieved further independence in 1931, the Gover-

---

29 Michael Bliss, *Confederation, A New Nationality*, page 79.

nor-General was selected by the Prime Minister of Canada.)

And, as part of his commitment to a strong central government, he got the federal parliament to have all the powers not specified as provincial as well as the authority to disallow any provincial act.

The Fathers of Confederation defined control of the nation of Canada by the formula, "Peace, Order and Good Government."

It is this introductory phrase of the British North America Act of 1867 that gave Parliament the authority to pass laws on matters not specifically given to the provinces. Contrast this with the 1776 American Declaration of Independence's " . . . life, liberty, and the pursuit of happiness."

Arrangements were made, too, for Prince Edward Island, Newfoundland, Rupert's Land and British Columbia to enter Confederation if they wished. There was much opposition in each of those areas. Indeed, even when Newfoundland joined in 1949, there was almost a riot by citizens opposed to Confederation.

The next step, after the seventy-two resolutions of the Constitution were agreed to by the Canadian Parliament by a vote of 91 in favor and 33 opposed, was to obtain approval from the Parliament in England.

The last of the three Confederation Conferences began on December 4, 1866. Macdonald was elected chairman of the London Conference and carefully negotiated the resolutions.

Macdonald was . . . an adroit and responsible chairman. Sir Frederick Rogers, the Permanent Under-Secretary of the Colonial Office . . . watched Macdonald with admiration as he steered some of the delicate compromises through the London Conference . . . 'He stated and argued the case with cool, ready fluency, while at the same time you saw that every word was measured, and that while he was making for a point ahead, he was never for a moment unconscious of the rocks among which he had to steer.[30]

---

30 P. B. Waite, *Macdonald: His Life and World* (1975), page 63.

In March of the next year the Conference ended and Queen Victoria signed Royal Assent.

The British North America Act of 1867 (known since 1982 as the Constitution Act) created a federation, dividing powers between the central government in Ottawa and the provincial governments. The federal authority had powers such as defence, post office, trade and commerce, currency, Indian affairs, criminal law and communications. The provinces had control over property, municipalities and education.

On July 1, 1867, the new Dominion of Canada was formed consisting of four provinces—Nova Scotia, New Brunswick, Quebec and Ontario. Newfoundland, Prince Edward Island and British Columbia did not join at that time. The latter province was negotiating on the promise of a railway to be built. Macdonald had realized earlier that only a powerful central government could undertake the costly and crucial task of building such a railway.

While Sir John was in Britain he and Queen Victoria made arrangements for a special Confederation medal. The design, by the engraver Joseph Shepherd Wyon, was approved by Macdonald and the Queen once they felt it was "in keeping with the historic dignity of the occasion."

The medal, three inches in diameter, bears a portrait of Queen Victoria on the obverse side. The reverse side shows an allegorical group of female figures. The leading figure, Britannia, with trident in right hand and her left hand resting on a lion, presents the Charter of Confederation to the four sister provinces joining together into the Dominion of Canada. The four sisters each hold an implement of livelihood, symbolizing the chief source of their respective province's wealth and economic activity. Ontario holds a sickle and sheaf of corn, Quebec a canoe paddle, Nova Scotia a miner's spade (for the Cape Breton coal fields) and New Brunswick a lumberman's axe. Encircling the whole scene is the motto, "Canada Reorganized 1867, Youth and Ancestral Vigour."

The only Confederation medal cast in gold was presented to the

Queen. Fifty medals were struck in silver for distribution amongst the Fathers of Confederation and high dignitaries. Finally, 500 medals were made of bronze for presentation to members of the House of Commons and the Senate, delegates to the Charlottetown and Quebec Conferences not present at the London Conference (whose attendees received silver issues), members of colonial parliaments before Confederation, and to approximately 100 institutions in Canada.[31]

If the reader knows where any of these medals may be purchased the author would appreciate a call.

Confederation certainly did not end all Macdonald's and Canada's difficulties. As the Prime Minister said in a letter to Sir John Rose, a Canadian lawyer and politician, in 1872, "Confederation is only yet the gristle, and it will require five years more before it hardens into bone."[32]

However, the first Canadian federal election took place between August 7 and September 20, 1867 with a voter turnout of 73.1 percent. Macdonald and his party took 100 out of 180 seats.

---

31 George Bolotenko, *A Future Defined*, page 182.
32 John Colombo, *Colombo's Canadian Quotations*, page 376.

CHAPTER FOUR

Sir John A. Macdonald's Political Life After Confederation

"They are to be purely a civil, not a military body,
with as little gold lace, fuss, and fine feathers as
possible, not a crack cavalry regiment, but an
efficient police force for the rough and ready—
particularly ready—enforcement of law and justice."
—*John A. Macdonald, House of Commons Debates;*
introducing the bill establishing the
North West Mounted Police, May 3, 1873

The opening of the first Canadian Parliament took place on November 7, 1867. Before legislation could be brought before the House of Commons and the Senate, a speaker had to be elected, the payment of members decided and standing committees appointed. In connection with money to members, Macdonald suggested, "$6.00 per day for session of about ninety days and ten cents a mile for travel expenses."

Another priority task for the government was the annexation of the western part of the country. Negotiations in London led to the Rupert's Land Act of 1868 which made a transfer of Rupert's Land and the North-Western Territory from the control of the Hudson's Bay Company to the Dominion of Canada. The company sold its rights for £300,000 (about 12 million dollars). It was an area larger than India. In 1870 the Manitoba Act created the province of Manitoba. Unfortunately, concerns of the Métis were all but forgotten. Louis Riel had led a protest in 1849 and announced in 1870 a Red

River provisional government. He wanted the Métis's own conditions for entry into the rest of Canada. An armed force of Canadians was imprisoned in Fort Garry by the Métis in 1870 and subsequently a Canadian, Thomas Scott, was executed by a Métis firing squad. Riel fled to the United States.

In 1884 Riel was invited to return to lead the Métis. Another small rebellion took place in which fatalities occurred on both sides. Troops from the East were transported via the nearly completed Canadian Pacific Railway and the Métis were defeated at Batoche. Riel was arrested and charged with treason.

Macdonald's Conservative government was caught between Catholic Quebec which sympathized with Riel and the rebels and Protestant Ontario which felt they both should be punished. It should be noted that Macdonald had given Riel three reprieves.

1885 brought about the hanging of Louis Riel. The execution created a storm of controversy and caused a split between the English in Ontario and the French in Quebec which lasted for decades. The House of Commons had supported the hanging by a vote of 130 to 50.

Not only were the Métis and aboriginals a problem but there was a need to provide law and order in the vast lands in the northwest. Sir John created, in 1873, the North-West Mounted Police (see quote page 46). According to Peter Waite, "Macdonald's N.W.M.P. was an inspired creation."[33] Members of the force were soldiers and police at the same time. Today, their descendants, now the R.C.M.P., are in most Canadian provinces.

In British Columbia, as we read, the gold rush of 1858 had brought many American miners who were supporters of a union with the United States. In addition, the Governor of British Columbia, Frederick Seymour, procrastinated over discussions of Confederation with Canada. He believed that a union was only desired by a minority of business people who were hoping the move would solve B.C.'s economic problems.

Macdonald became upset at Seymour's resistance to joining Canada.

---

33 Peter Waite, *The Illustrated History of Canada*, page 350.

The Prime Minister stated in a letter that Seymour should be recalled, "as being perfectly unfit for his present position under present circumstances. From all I hear, he was never fit for it."[34]

In 1869, Governor Seymour died at Bella Bella on the B.C. coast from dysentery, excessive imbibing or both.

The next year a delegation from B.C. came to Ottawa to discuss terms of a union. It was agreed that Canada would take over B.C.'s debt and that a transcontinental railway would be finished within ten years. On July 20, 1871, British Columbia officially entered Confederation.

The railway was an immense task requiring large sums of money. Sir John obtained a promise that Britain would guarantee 2,500,000 pounds sterling.

The Liberal leader, Alexander Mackenzie, called it "an act of insane recklessness and one of the most foolish things that could be imagined."[35]

Another problem for Sir John occurred in 1871 when he travelled to Washington to negotiate a fisheries treaty and obtain tariff concessions with the United States. Unfortunately, the British representatives wanted to avoid any problems with the Americans and the resulting Treaty of Washington gave little to Canada. Fishing rights were sold to the U.S., no American money was give to recompence Canada for the Fenian raids and there were no reciprocal trade agreements.

Macdonald suffered politically because of the Treaty but in the long run it brought better relations between Canada and the United States.

On May 3, 1872, John A. spoke in the House of Commons about the Washington Treaty:

When someone writes my biography—if I am ever thought worthy of having such an interesting document prepared—and when, as a matter of history, the questions connected with this Treaty are upheld, it

---

34 Pierre Berton, *The National Dream*, page 6.

35 *Dictionary of Canadian Biography*, Vol. 9, 1861–1870, page 715.

will be found that, upon this, as well as upon every other point, I did all I could to protect the rights and claims of the Dominion.[36]

In that same year Macdonald obtained passage of the Dominion Lands Act by which the policy of granting free land to settlers was established in Manitoba and the Northwest.

Another federal election happened in August and September of 1872. One of the issues was trade unionism. Macdonald had earlier worked to eradicate the law criminalizing membership in trade unions and also introduced legislation that strengthened the union's position.

As a token of appreciation a group of trade unionists gave Lady Macdonald a gift. Sir John thanked the working men on Agnes's behalf and said,

I am a working man myself. I know that I work more than nine hours every day myself; then I think that I am a practical mechanic. If you look at the Confederation Act, in the forming of which I had some hand, you will admit that I am a pretty good joiner and cabinet maker.[37]

It was during that September 1872 election that Hugh Allen of the Merchant's bank in Montreal supplied Macdonald and the Conservative Party with campaign funds. Allen contributed a total of $350,000 to Conservative candidates with $45,000 of it going to Sir John. This was ostensibly in exchange for Allen to become president of the transcontinental railway. An incriminating telegram by Macdonald to Allen was later made public. It read, "I must have another ten thousand. Will be the last time of calling. Do not fail me. Answer today." This resulted in the so-called Pacific Scandal.

In 1873, Parliament resumed with severe criticism of Prime Minister Macdonald over the scandal. In defence, Sir John stated that he had not used Allan's money for his own election but it was used for

36 Peter Newman, *The John A. Macdonald Album*, page 99.
37 Donald Swainson, *Macdonald of Kingston*, page 101.

various dinners and for bringing voters to the polls. As W. L. Morton states, "Elections had always been corrupt in North America, with bribery, treating and promises of patronage."[38]

Macdonald had felt in the election of 1872 that his opponents were opposed to Confederation and that they would weaken a strong central government. The railway, in his point of view, was vital to Confederation. The ends justified the means, he felt.

The Pacific Scandal was not a calculated corruption on Macdonald's part but showed a reckless carelessness in electioneering. George Cartier, Macdonald's co-leader, had also accepted large donations from Allan.

It is difficult today to understand how Sir John's morality in politics was evil. As has been said, at that time bribery and corruption were widespread. He at no time denied that he participated. He and many others used patronage to help win elections. He had used it with the purpose of uniting the Conservative Party and building the Canadian nation. He always denied that he personally benefited financially from these arrangements and the evidence supports this.

It is also true that patronage, cronyism and corruption still exist to a lesser degree in federal politics. Former Prime Minister Mulroney, former Prime Minister Chrétien and former Prime Minister Paul Martin have all been accused of unscrupulous actions.

A *Global Integrity* report for 2007 criticized Canada's judicial system, citing the government's executive hold over quasi-judicial appointments and the absence of rules around gifts offered to the judiciary.

In 2008, there were charges and counter-charges of violations of the Elections Act in the 2006 election. Elections Canada decided that sixty-four Conservative candidates had violated spending restrictions by using "in and out" bookkeeping.

Then too, the 2008 appointment of fifteen senators by Prime Minister Harper with seven being defeated Conservative candidates shows patronage is still part of the Canadian political system.

---

38 W. L. Morton, *The Critical Years, 1857-1873*, page 270.

In any event Macdonald tried to explain his reasons in a letter to the Governor-General Lord Dufferin.

It was therefore of importance, to his [Sir Hugh Allan's] interests and the undertaking with which he had so connected himself, that a Parliament favourable to such enterprises, and to the development of the country thereby, should be elected, and, as a man of business, he expended his money accordingly. And it suited the purposes of the Ministerial party to accept his subscriptions, as well as the subscriptions of others . . .

Our misfortune was that, by the base betrayal of these private communications, the names of certain members of the Government, including myself, were mixed up in the obtaining of these subscriptions. Had this betrayal not taken place, it would have been only known that Sir Hugh Allan, and the railways with which he had been connected, had taken a decided line in supporting one party in preference to another, by their influence and money.[39]

Dufferin did not condemn Macdonald but advised him to resign. The former wrote:

I believe there is no one in the country capable of administering its affairs to greater advantage than yourself. It is to you in fact that Canada owes its existence and your name will be preserved in History as the Father and Founder of the Dominion.[40]

Macdonald continued to fight. After speaking in the House of Commons for nearly five hours he finished his back-to-the-wall speech with these words.

I leave it to this House with every confidence. I am equal to either

---

39 Glen Finkel, *Winners and Losers, Canadian National Development 1867-1900*, page 32.

40 W. L. Morton, *The Critical Years, 1857-1873*, page 270.

fortune. I can see past the decision of this House either for or against me; but whether it be for or against me, I know—and it is no vain boast for me to say so, for even my enemies will admit that I am no boaster—that there does not exist in this country a man who has given more of his time, more of his heart, more of his wealth, or more of his intellect and power, such as they may be, for the good of this Dominion of Canada.[41]

In spite of this the pressure of the opposition continued and resulted in Macdonald resigning as Prime Minister in November of 1873. Less than twenty-four hours later his caucus members declared him their leader again.

Two months after the 1873 resignation, Liberal leader Alexander Mackenzie won a majority in the election and became Prime Minister. John A. kept his seat by winning in Kingston by thirty-seven votes over his opponent. The conservatives were reduced to sixty-seven in a 206 seat House of Commons.

After being charged with bribery in this election, John A. was cleared but his seat was declared vacant. In a by-election the same year he won Kingston again by only seventeen votes and became the leader of the opposition.

Unfortunately for Mackenzie, there was a Depression and slower trade reduced Canada's income. He told British Columbia that the railway would be put on hold indefinitely. In 1878 the B.C. provincial legislature resolved to secede from Canada unless construction to the coast began in 1881.

Macdonald proposed a National Policy which would introduce high tariffs to protect Canada's industries from foreign competition. In the election campaign of 1878 a vigorous Sir John staged a comeback. A portion of this involved a picnic in Toronto where 7000 persons were present. He said in part at that event:

> *. . . My opponents may talk about the Pacific Scandal; but Sir Hugh*

---

41 Pope, page 194.

Allan subscribed to the election fund out of his own money, and not out of the public chest . . . The Grits thought, when they formulated this charge, that they had got me down, and forever—(cries of "never")—but, gentlemen, I was exactly like that child's toy called jack-in-the-box, for as soon as the hands were taken off the lid up popped John A. (Loud laughter.) . . .[42]

Under Macdonald's National Policy his battle-cry for the election was "Canada for Canadians." It was more than just protective tariffs. It was a declaration of Canadian economic independence. The Conservative Party swept the general election.

Sir John A.'s National Policy Resolution was moved in the House of Commons, March 12, 1878:

That it be resolved that this house is of the opinion that the welfare of Canada required the adoption of a national policy which, by a judicious readjustment of the tariff, will benefit and foster the agricultural, the mining, the manufacturing and other interests of the Dominion; that such a policy will retain in Canada thousands of our fellow-countrymen now obliged to expatriate themselves in search of the employment denied them at home, will restore prosperity to our struggling industries now so sadly depressed, will prevent Canada from being made a sacrifice market, will encourage and develop an active inter-provincial trade, and moving (as it ought to do) in the direction of a reciprocity of tariffs with our neighbours, so far as the varied interests of Canada may demand, will greatly tend to procure for this country, a reciprocity of trade.[43]

Shortly after the government's implementation of this National Policy, Sir John jested that,

Trade revived, crops were abundant and bank stocks once more

---

42 Edwin Guillet, *You'll Never Die John A.*, page 182.
43 Peter Newman, *Renegade in Power*, page 147.

became buoyant, owing to the confidence of the people of Canada in the new Administration.

A citizen of Toronto assured me," continued Sir John with a straight face, "that his Conservative cow gave three quarts of milk more a day after the election than before; while a good Conservative lady friend solemnly affirmed that her hens laid more eggs, larger eggs, fresher eggs and more to the dozen ever since the new Administration came in.[44]

The Conservatives under Macdonald fought the National Policy through three more general elections, 1882, 1887, and 1891. They also appealed to the electorate using the slogan: "The old flag, the old policy and the old leader."

Construction of the transcontinental railway was recommenced in 1881 and finally completed in 1885. Because of the immensity of the undertaking, the railway received another $25,000,000 and a land grant of 25,000,000 acres. Sir John insisted the route be all Canadian. Stephen Leacock said the railway "was one of the greatest triumphs of our history."[45]

It should be understood that without Macdonald, there would have been no transcontinental railway by the all-Canadian route, north of Lake Superior, across the Prairies and through the Canadian Rockies to the Pacific Ocean. He knew that it was essential to hold British Columbia and the Prairie Provinces against advancing American settlement.

Sir John had become a symbol of Canadian government and the Conservative Party but also a symbol of Canada itself. He had magical personal charm, cheerfulness and buoyant optimism. He also was politically prudent in choosing his cabinet which took in a number of Liberals of Ontario, Bleus of Quebec, and Reformers of New Brunswick. Although he was not an orator like Lincoln or Churchill, he was able to convince his listeners and win elections.

---

44 Donald Swainson, *Macdonald of Kingston*, page 125.
45 Stephen Leacock, *Canada: The Foundations of Its Future*, page 182.

Biographers are agreed that John A. Macdonald had an exceptional memory. He had the rare ability to remember names and faces. He also, because of constant reading, was able to quote authors like Charles Dickens and politicians like Disraeli and Gladstone.

Combined with the above talents was the fact that Macdonald worked harder at more political things than any of his opponents. According to his secretary, Sir John "allowed himself no relaxation from the daily task of administering the affairs of the Dominion."[46]

In 1883 a biographer J. Collins wrote

The influence of Sir John Macdonald's career upon the political life of the country, and upon public opinion, has been greater and better, and of a nature that will prove enduring, than that of any other Canadian statesman, whether dead or living.[47]

Macdonald realized early in his political career that the French-English duality must be respected as one of the essential aspects of any constitutional arrangement and governance.

He became the indispensable man without whom Canada might have disintegrated.

In 1884 Queen Victoria conferred a further honour on the Prime Minister.

10 Downing Street, Whitehall,
November 15, 1884
Dear Sir J. Macdonald,
In acknowledgment of your long and distinguished service Her Majesty graciously authorizes me to propose to you that you should receive the honour of a Grand Cross of the Bath.
Believe me to remain

---

46 Pope, page 638.
47 J. E. Collins, *Life and Times of the Right Honourable Sir John A. Macdonald*, page 500.

Faithfully yours,
W.E. Gladstone
To which Sir John replied:—
Batt's Hotel, Dover Street
November 15, 1884
Dear Mr. Gladstone,
I have the honour to acknowledge the receipt of your note of to-day, informing me that the Queen has graciously authorized you to propose to me that I should receive the honour of a Grand Cross of the Bath.

I gratefully accept this distinguished mark of Her Majesty's favour, and I am especially gratified that this announcement should be made through you, and the honour conferred through your kind intervention.

Believe me to be, dear Mr. Gladstone,
Faithfully yours,
John A. Macdonald[48]

At a reception in Toronto in 1884 to celebrate Sir John's forty years in Parliament he said,

> *. . . This is not only a great and glorious incident but it is also a very solemn one. When I look back through my forty years of public life; when I remember how few remain of those who with me entered full of hope, life, and the earnestness of youth; when I bear in mind that those who do remain are like myself, feeble old men—(cries of 'No, no!' and a voice, 'You'll never die, John A.!')—when I think of all this, feelings of a most solemn nature awake in my mind . . . I heard a cry just now from one of my friends saying 'You will never die!' (Laughter.) Gentlemen, I really do believe that those who are in political opposition to me think so too—(renewed laughter)— and I fear, though they pray for me and all other like sinners, that in the supplications there is no pious expression of the desire that my life may be long spared. (Loud laughter.) They have no objection that I should go*

48 Pope, page 175.

to another and a better world, and that I should not prolong my stay in this one. (Loud laughter.) I am happy, gentlemen, to state to you that your good wishes with respect to the renewal and the continuance of my health have been to a very great extent realized. (Loud cheering.) Thanks to a good conscience . . . I come back to you nearly as good as new—(cheers and laughter)—a little worse for the wear, to be sure—(laughter)—but still able to stand the battle for a few years longer. (Cheers.) I was much amused, gentlemen, when in England to read a sentence in a Toronto newspaper, stating that the position of the Opposition was simply this: 'If Sir John A.'s stomach gives in, then the Opposition will go in—(loud laughter)—but if John A.'s stomach holds out, then we will stay out.' (Continued laughter.) You will be glad to know that there are strong indications that they will stay out. (Hear, hear!)[49]

In 1891 Sir John was seventy-six years old but he fought the election that year just as he had in his younger years. His supporters wanted him to appear in as many constituencies as possible, even in snowstorms and freezing rain, and he forced his tired body to do so. The election was on March 5, 1891.

The result was another victory for the Conservatives. Later Prime Minister Macdonald had the satisfaction of sitting in the House of Commons with his son Hugh who had been elected in Winnipeg. The date was April 29, 1891.

It was during that session of Parliament that Sir John was criticized in the House of Commons for his cab fare to and from Parliament in the previous session which had amounted to $134.00. He replied as follows:

I am sorry the Honourable Gentleman objects to that item. I do myself . . . but my limbs are weary and weak. I cannot walk . . . After half a century of active work, it does seem hard that I am not to be allowed to ride for business purposes . . . In the winter I took a cab

---

49 Edwin Guillet, *You'll Never Die, John A.*, page 90.

from my house to Parliament, but I economized last summer by riding
in a bus instead of Buckley's cab. But the buses are too cold for my feet
in winter and I get a cab now . . . As long as I am [Prime Minister],
the overburdened tax-payers will have to pay my cab hire. I think they
will be quite willing.[50]

Less than a month later in 1891 Sir John's secretary, Joseph Pope, noticed something wrong with Sir John's speech. This was the beginning of a series of strokes which culminated with a final one on June 6 which was fatal.

John A. Macdonald had been Prime Minister of Canada for nineteen years making him second only to Mackenzie-King as the longest serving Prime Minister of Canada. He is the only Canadian Prime Minister to win six majority governments and is the only Prime Minister to die in office while holding that position. He had led the Conservative Party for twenty-four years (1867 to 1891).

He had been central to major Canadian political events such as the Riel Rebellion, the Pacific Scandal, the building of the transcontinental railway, the National Policy and most importantly Confederation.

He has been rightly called the "Father of Confederation," the "Chief Architect of Confederation," the "Father of His Country," the "Builder of Our Nation," and the "Man Who Made Us."

---

50 Lena Newman, *The John A. Macdonald Album*, page 204.

CHAPTER FIVE

The Death of John A. Macdonald

"During my long public service of nearly half a century, I have been true to my country and its best interests."

—*Ottawa, February 17, 1891*

As we read, during the 1891 election Macdonald became exhausted and was taken ill at the end of February. His last message to the people of Canada was issued on February 7 from his home, Earnscliffe. Parts of this communication follow:

To the Electors of Canada:

In soliciting at your hands a renewal of the confidence which I have enjoyed, as a Minister of the Crown, for thirty years, it is, I think, convenient that I should take advantage of the occasion to define the attitude of the Government, in which I am First Minister, towards the leading political issues of the day.

As in 1878, in 1882, and again in 1887, so in 1891, do questions relating to the trade and commerce of the country occupy a foremost place in the public mind. Our policy in respect thereto is to-day what it has been for the past thirteen years, and is directed by a firm determination to foster and develop the varied resources of the Dominion, by every means in our power, consistent with Canada's position as an integral portion of the British Empire. To that end we have laboured in the past, and we propose to continue in the work to which we have applied ourselves, of building up on this continent, under the flag of England, a great and powerful nation.

When, in 1878, we were called upon to administer the affairs of the Dominion, Canada occupied a position in the eyes of the world very different from that which she enjoys to-day. At that time a profound depression hung like a pall over the whole country, from the Atlantic Ocean to the western limits of the province of Ontario, beyond which to the Rocky Mountains stretched a vast and almost unknown wilderness. Trade was depressed, manufactures languished, and, exposed to ruinous competition, Canadians were fast sinking into the position of being mere hewers of wood and drawers of water for the great nation dwelling to the south of us. We determined to change this unhappy state of things. We felt that Canada, with its agricultural resources, rich in its fisheries, timber, and mineral wealth, was worthy of a nobler position than that of being a slaughter market for the United States. We said to the Americans: 'We are perfectly willing to trade with you on equal terms. We are desirous of having a fair reciprocity treaty, but we will not consent to open our markets to you while yours remain closed to us.' So we inaugurated the National Policy. You all know what followed. Almost as if by magic, the whole face of the country underwent a change. Stagnation and apathy and gloom—ay, and want and misery too—gave place to activity and enterprise and prosperity. The miners of Nova Scotia took courage; the manufacturing industries in our great centres revived and multiplied; the farmer found a market for his produce, the artisan and labourer employment at good wages, and all Canada rejoiced under the quickening impulse of a new-found life. The age of deficits was past, and an overflowing treasury gave to the Government the means of carrying forward those great works necessary to the realization of our purpose to make this country a homogenous whole . . .

Under the broad folds of the Union Jack, we enjoy the most ample liberty to govern ourselves as we please, and at the same time we participate in the advantages which flow from association with the mightiest Empire the world has ever seen. Not only are we free to manage our domestic concerns, but, practically, we possess the privilege of making our own treaties with foreign countries, and, in our relations with the outside world, we enjoy the prestige inspired by a consciousness of the fact that behind us towers the majesty of England. The question which you will shortly be called upon to determine resolves itself into this: shall we endanger our possession of the great heritage bequeathed to us by our fathers, and submit ourselves to direct taxation for the privilege of having our tariff fixed at Washington, with a prospect of ultimately becoming a portion of the American Union? I commend these issues to your determination, and to the judgment of the whole people of Canada, with an unclouded confidence that you will proclaim to the world your resolve to show yourselves not unworthy of the proud distinction that you enjoy, of being numbered among the most dutiful and loyal subjects of our beloved Queen.

As for myself, my course is clear. A British subject I was born—a British subject I will die. With my utmost effort, with my latest breath, will I oppose the 'veiled treason' which attempts by sordid means and mercenary proffers to lure our people from their allegiance. During my long public service of nearly half a century, I have been true to my country and its best interests, and I appeal with equal confidence to the man who have trusted me in the past, and to the young hope of the country, with whom rests its destinies for the future, to give me their united and strenuous aid in this, my last effort, for the unity of the Empire and the preservation of our commercial and political freedom.

I remain, gentlemen,
Your faithful servant,
John A. Macdonald[51]

The last letter sent by Sir John before his death was published in the *Victoria Colonist* and was written to the Premier of British Columbia, John Robson.

---

51 Pope, pages 772-77.

Earnscliffe, Ottawa

May 19, 1891

My Dear Robson,—It has occurred to me that the present would be an opportune season for your Government to discuss with ours the various questions still unsettled between us.

You, I presume can get away from Victoria with little or no inconvenience, and you will find us here in Parliamentary session until the 1st of July or later. We will then scatter until October, and at that season you, I suppose, will be wanted at home.

Besides it will be a pleasant season for your journey—so, give yourself leave of absence, and . . . you and I can take up . . . and any other unsolved questions that may remain. Herein fail not.

Yours sincerely,

John A. Macdonald[52]

Four days later from the date of the above letter, a severe stroke paralyzed his right side and destroyed his ability to speak. Doctors thought his condition was hopeless.

Word of his pending death spread throughout Canada. Bells were taken off the horse drawn street-cars that passed Earnscliffe. Boats on the Ottawa River stopped blowing their whistles and slowed their engines as they approached the cliff below Earnscliffe.

Medical bulletins were issued periodically which revealed Sir John's weakening situation.

> *June 4, 6:45 p.m. Sir John Macdonald's condition throughout the day has been simply one of continuous weakness from a deficient heart action.*
>
> *June 4, 11 p.m. Sir John is still conscious and makes known his needs through a pressure of his left hand.*
>
> *June 5, 2 p.m. Sir John's hours of life are steadily waning.*
>
> *June 5, 7 p.m. Sir John's end is fast approaching.*

---

52 Adam Mercer, *The Life and Career of the Right Honourable Sir John A. Macdonald*, page 544.

June 6, 10:30 p.m. Sir John died this evening at quarter past ten o'clock.[53]

Joseph Pope, his secretary, went to the gate of Earnscliffe and announced to reporters, "Gentlemen, Sir John Macdonald is dead."

On Sunday morning June 7 the body of the late Prime Minister lay in the hall at Earnscliffe. The stone residence was draped in purple and white. The Governor General, Sir John's ministers and close friends filed in singly for a special farewell.

Two days later, the body was then moved to the Senate Chamber of Parliament and thousands walked past all day and into the night.

The following day a funeral procession went through crowded Ottawa streets to St. Albans Anglican Church which Sir John had attended.

After the service the body was taken to the railway station and placed on a CPR funeral train to go to Kingston.

The late Sir John again lay in state on June 11 in the City Hall of Kingston. He was then buried at Cataraqui Cemetery where his mother, his father, his first wife, infant son and two sisters were also buried.

On that day, all shops in Kingston were closed, buildings draped and church bells tolled.

Today, the Cataraqui Cemetery is a five minutes walk from the Kingston railway station.

Sir Wilfred Laurier, Macdonald's adversary in Parliament, gave the former Prime Minister's eulogy in the House of Commons on June 8, 1891. Part of his speech follows:

For my part, I say with all truth, his loss overwhelms me, and it also overwhelms this Parliament, as if indeed on one of the institutions of the land had given way. Sir John Macdonald now belongs to the ages, and it can be said with certainty, that the career which has just been closed is one of the most remarkable careers of this century. It would be

---

53 Newman, page 208.

premature at this time to attempt to fix or anticipate what will be the final judgment of history upon him, but there were in his career and in his life, features so prominent and so conspicuous that already they shine with a glow which time cannot alter, which even now appear before the eye such as they will appear to the end in history. I think it can be asserted that for the supreme art of governing men, Sir John Macdonald was gifted as few men in any land or in any age were gifted, gifted with the most high of all qualities, qualities which would have made him famous wherever exercised and which would have shone all the more conspicuously the larger the theatre. The fact that he could congregate together elements the most heterogeneous and blend them into one compact party, and to the end of his life keep them steadily under his hand, is perhaps altogether unprecedented. The fact that during all those years he retained unimpaired not only the confidence, but the devotion—the ardent devotion and affection of his party, is evidence that besides those higher qualities of statesmanship to which we were the daily witnesses, he was also endowed with those inner, subtle, undefinable graces of soul which win and keep the hearts

Macdonald's grave at Kingston's Cataraqui Cemetery.

of men. As to his statesmanship, it is written in the history of Canada. It may be said without any exaggeration whatever, that the life of Sir John Macdonald, from the date he entered Parliament, is the history of Canada, for he was connected and associated with all the events, all the facts which brought Canada from the position Canada then occupied—the position of two small provinces, having nothing in common but a common allegiance, united by a bond of paper, and united by nothing else—to the present state of development which Canada has reached . . .

We remember that his actions always displayed great originality of view, unbounded fertility of resources, a high level of intellectual conception, and, above all, a far reaching vision beyond the events of the day, and still higher, permeating the whole, a broad patriotism, a devotion to Canada's welfare, Canada's advancement and Canada's glory.[54]

---

54 Cynthia Smith and Jack McLeod, *Sir John A.*, pages 178-79.

CHAPTER SIX

The Legacies of John A. Macdonald

"If I had any influence of the minds of the people of Canada, any power over their intellect, I would leave them this legacy: 'Whatever you do adhere to the Union—we are a great country, and shall become one of the greatest in the universe if we persevere; we shall sink into significance and adversity if we suffer it to be broken.' God and nature have made the two Canadas one—let no factious men be allowed to put them asunder."

—John A. Macdonald
Speech 1867

The greatest legacy (something that has come down to us) of Macdonald is, of course, Confederation. The road to this miraculous achievement was extremely rough and it needed someone with determination, vision, and skill to achieve it. John A. was that person. He was truly a giant among the men of his time.

This chapter deals with other tangible items, many of which exist today. We begin with statues sculpted and erected to commemorate his achievements:

Prime Minister John Thompson delivered a speech in 1893 when the first statue of Sir John was unveiled in Hamilton, Ontario, at Gore Park.

I have unveiled the image of one of the most illustrious men of our generation. I have spoken of this being the first statue erected to his honour in Canada, but before it had been erected his bust had been unveiled in the cathedral of St. Paul's in the heart of England, as the memorial of one whose services to the Empire deserved to be ranked with those of Wellington and Nelson . . . As time goes on other statues will be raised to his memory in various parts of Canada, and yet the grandest thing for his memory will be that his fame needs no monument to extend or to preserve it. At the time of his death it was poetically and truthfully said, 'His work—a nation—stands as his monument.' Of no man or any period can it be more truly said that he was the father and founder of his country . . .

He was ambitious in the best sense of the word. He was ambitious to infuse into the minds of his countrymen sentiments and ideas which were wider than the issues of party—ambitious to make Canada great—ambitious to silence the voice of faction and the noise of discord—ambitious to leave this country and the Empire better off for the toils and sacrifices of his life . . .

In his long parliamentary career how well justified are those words of his . . . 'I know that in the long career of political life I have made many mistakes, that the Government of which I am a member has, of course, made errors and been guilty of omission as well as commission; but I can honestly say that the desire was good and the motive was good.'

I thank you, citizens of Hamilton, for the noble work which you have done in erecting the first statue to Sir John Macdonald.[55]

Ten years earlier, a statue of George Etienne-Cartier was the first monument to be placed on Parliament Hill. Sir John had recommended that it be placed there.

In 1895 a bronze statue of Sir John by Hébert was erected outside the eastern end of the Parliament Buildings in Ottawa. It is placed high on a granite pedestal and he is shown as an orator looking over the city with a text of his speech in his hand.

In the same year (1895) as the statue of Sir John at the Parliament

---

55 Pope, pages 784-787.

Statue of Macdonald on Ottawa's Parliament Hill

Buildings, another imposing bronze was unveiled at the Place du Canada in Montreal in front of the Basilica, Mary Queen of the World.

Other eastern statues of Macdonald are at Adolphustown, Ontario, St. Patrick in Quebec and a monument in front of Queen's Park in Toronto.

Victoria, British Columbia, has a larger than life statue of Sir John which stands outside the city hall on Douglas Street. It was unveiled on July 1, 1982. Although the federal election of 1878 resulted in his Conservative Party's return as government, Macdonald lost his seat in Kingston. He was still Prime Minister and was elected by acclamation in Victoria even though he had not been there.

Kingston, of course, has many Macdonald remnants including a large statue of him in the city park erected in 1895.

There are also a number of buildings that he occupied over decades. His residences reflected his economic and social standing in the community. In his early years the home on Rideau Street (page 18).

As we read in Chapter One, his first law office in 1835 was Wellington Street, a second larger office on King Street (1849 to 1860) and a third on Clarence Street. The desk that he used in his law office is on display at the Fort Henry museum in Kingston.

Macdonald's Kingston homes include a home he had built on Brock Street which no longer exists. Next was Bellevue House (1848-1849) which is restored to the 1840s period and open to the public. Their brief stay at this rented home was unhappy because Isabella was confined to her sick room and their infant son died a month after they occupied the house.

Bellevue proved too expensive for John A. and he moved to

Johnston Street where his second son Hugh was born. Another home for Macdonald was Heathfield on the outside of Kingston. He lived there only when he visited that city and although it was used from 1865 to 1876 it was not a significant part of his life. Later Macdonald rented a home on Wellingston Street (1876-1878) and also rented a dwelling on Earl Street for his sister (1878 to 1889)

All these buildings have bronze plaques marking the association with him.

In all, Macdonald had nearly twenty-five changes of residence in Kingston, partly because of domestic situations with his mother, sisters, in-laws, and wife. These houses also served as his legal residence for purposes of his representation as M.P. for Kingston.

After the seat of government was transferred to Ottawa in 1865 Macdonald also had residences in that city. He first lived in a row house at the corner of Daly and Cumberland Streets. It was called the "Quadrilateral" by Macdonald. He lived there after his second marriage until 1872. Unfortunately, the home was destroyed by fire in 1873 and not even a plaque marks the site today.

They moved to a house on Chapel Street (1873 to 1876) which was later replaced with other buildings and has again no plaque to identify the area and its relationship to Sir John.

From 1878 to 1883 they resided in palatial Stadacona Hall (the name comes from a 16th century aboriginal village near present day Quebec City which Jacques Cartier reached in 1535). It is located at 395 Laurier Avenue.

John A. moved from it in 1883 as he purchased the home called Earnscliffe at that time. No belongings of his remain at Stadacona Hall as far as is known.

Macdonald's statue in Victoria,

Macdonald's statue in Kingston's City Park.

Stadacona Hall was built in 1871 and after World War Two was purchased by Belgium for the Belgium ambassador. It was put on the market for $1.7 million in 1995 and was bought by the country of Brunei Darussalem in Borneo which uses it for its high commission office.

Kingston has the Cataraqui Cemetery where Sir John is buried. To mark his grave there is a cast-iron Victorian railing surrounding a plot with a small granite monument. Every year since 1891 there has been a commemorative service at the cemetery. In most years a keynote speaker has been invited to talk on some aspect of Macdonald's contribution to Canada.

Overseas in London, St. Paul's Cathedral has a bust of Sir John as mentioned earlier by P.M. John Thompson. Westminster Abbey also has a monument to him.

At the London Conference held at the Westminster Hotel in 1866-1867 where the terms of Confederation were agreed to and the British North America Act was drafted, there was a plaque placed in the Conference Room. The building has since been demolished but the plaque has been preserved, moved from London, and is now in the west block of the Parliament Buildings (see page 73).

Today, one of the most enduring symbols of our nation is Parliament Hill and the Gothic parliament buildings situated on it. The Library at the back and the East Block were the only sections of the Parliament Buildings not destroyed by fire in 1916. Macdonald's office in the East Block has been restored just as it was in 1872. He was the only prime minister to use this office.

As the guides will tell you there are a few items in this room that were there in Macdonald's time. There is a secretary/bookcase

Macdonald's rented Kingston home called Bellevue.

which was a gift from supporters and which Macdonald had in his study at Earnscliffe. The words Dominion Secretory are carved on the drawer between the desk and the bookcase and are a play on the word secretary and Sir John's Tory politics.

The room was heated by a coal fireplace which was lit before Sir John arrived in the mornings. A map of Canada in 1871 hangs on the wall. His tartan scarf and top hat are hung on pegs by the door.

On the desk lies a paper condemning Louis Riel and the Order in Council stating, "that the law be allowed to take its course with Louis Riel convicted of high treason." Beside it is the telegram confirming the execution had taken place.

The only water in the room came from a corner sink fed by a cold water gravity tank on the roof. It still works so the guide said. A curtain hangs beside it which Macdonald could pull around him for a quick change or a sponge bath.

Another office is that of George-Etienne Cartier. All prime ministers beginning with Wilfred Laurier in 1896 used this office until

Macdonald's Ottawa rented home called Stadacona Hall (2009).

Pierre Trudeau moved the Prime Minister's Office to the Langevin Building in 1976.

There is also the office of the Governor General commencing with Lord Dufferin who was there from 1872 to 1878 and the privy council chamber where the cabinet met from 1872 to 1876.

These are interesting tourist attractions but little original furniture is present. The building is open to the public only in the summer.

In 1965 a bridge was constructed connecting Ottawa to Gatineau, Quebec. It was named the Macdonald-Cartier Bridge. The name is representative of the link between French and English Canada.

There is also an Ontario highway called the Macdonald-Cartier Freeway (401).

In 1928 an airport was opened south of Ottawa. It has been enlarged and modernized since then and is now known as the "Ottawa Macdonald-Cartier International Airport."

There are many schools across Canada named after Sir John and Macdonald is depicted on the Canadian ten dollar bill.

In 2008 the Library and Archives of Canada has promoted an online exhibition called "Sir John A. Macdonald: Canada's Patriot Statesman." It contains papers (220,000 pages), photographs, books

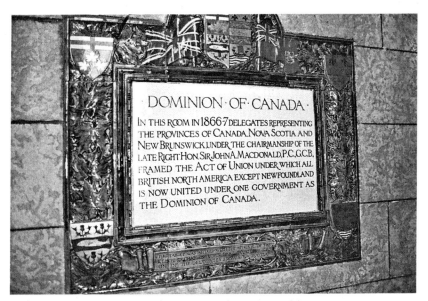

London plaque. Now in Canada's Parliament Building.

and published materials, art and ephemera on Macdonald.[56] Peter Newman writes the following about former Prime Minister Diefenbaker who felt he (the P.M.) was the twentieth century successor to Macdonald.

At his office in [Parliament], Diefenbaker worked under a portrait and beside a full-figure statuette of Macdonald. His inkwell had once belonged to Sir John A. In the Privy council chamber, Diefenbaker sat in Macdonald's original chair, and dried the signature on his instructions with Sir John's spring blotter. One of Macdonald's mantel clocks timed his movements and had to be carted to whichever of his three Parliament Hill offices Diefenbaker was occupying. In his official residence, at 24 Sussex Drive, Diefenbaker encircled himself even more liberally with Macdonald relics, including parts of his library, many portraits of him, his easy chair, another clock, and a medallion given to a barber who had once shaved Sir John. The most valuable item in the collection was a copy,

---

56 www.collectionscanada.gc.ca/sir-john-a-macdonald/index-e.html.

in Macdonald's own handwriting, of the original National Policy,
drawn up on January 16, 1878, at a political meeting in Toronto's
Shaftesbury Hall.[57]

Diefenbaker also had a ten volume edition of the works of Moliere that had been in Sir John's library at Earnscliffe and still had the latter's book mark.

All such memorabilia should be collected by the Canadian government and put on display for the public.

The legacy of Sir John's home called Earnscliffe merits a separate chapter.

57 Peter Newman, *Renegade in Power*, page 185.

CHATPER SEVEN

John A. Macdonald and Earnscliffe

"It is the house that Sir John A. Macdonald made famous."

—*Norman Reddaway*[58]

Of all the tangible reminders of the life of Sir John A. Macdonald, this author feels the house called Earnscliffe is the most significant.

To begin with it was named by him. Sir John's invalid daughter Mary told a story about her father visiting the Reynolds who owned Earnscliffe and found the family discussing a name for the house. They were thinking of Eaglescliffe and Sir John was said to have suggested the old English world for eagle—earn. His idea was accepted.

Our first prime minister lived there for nine years until his death in this house in 1891.

Earnscliffe is also intertwined with the history of Ottawa.

After the War of 1812 the British Government decided to try to obtain a navigable waterway from the Ottawa River to Kingston as a defence measure against the United States. This route was called the Rideau Canal. (The word *rideau* is French for curtain and refers to the appearance of the falls on the Hull side when Samuel de Champlain travelled up the Ottawa River in 1613.)

58 Norman Reddaway, *Earnscliffe*, (Commonwealth Relations Office) London, page 1.

Earnscliffe, 1891.

Earnscliffe, today.

In 1826 Lieutenant Colonel John By of the Royal Engineers was put in charge. One of his contractors was Thomas McKay who constructed the bridge from Hull to Bytown (Ottawa). This was the first bridge to link Upper and Lower Canada.

McKay also built a warehouse at the Ottawa entrance to the canal which still stands today as the Bytown Museum.

The author of Earnscliffe, Norman Reddaway, writes

McKay is said, by the speed and skill of his work, and by his shrewdness to have made a very substantial profit on his Canal contract. One story has it that Colonel By, in awarding the contract to McKay, had assumed that the stone for the lock masonry would have to come from across the river in Hull. McKay, however, dug down in Major's Hill Park, close to the locks, and discovered stone which he claimed to be of a quality identical with the Hull stone. After some hesitation Colonel By is said to have agreed to the use of the Major's Hill Park stone. McKay's gain from eliminating much of his transport charges must have been considerable.[59]

McKay built eight Ottawa locks. After the Canal was completed in 1832 McKay built Rideau Hall in 1838 which was later sold in 1866 to the Canadian Government as the official home of the Governor General. This building with improvements is still the official residence of the Governor General of Canada.

McKay also acquired the land where Earnscliffe was built by his son-in-law John Mackinnon. The name Sir John later gave the house is symbolic. Earnscliffe is perched on the edge of the cliff above the Ottawa river like an eagle eyeing the scene below it and the Laurentian Hills beyond. Today it is just east of the Macdonald-Cartier Bridge. The address is 140 Sussex Drive and the home can be clearly seen from the Ottawa River. It could not be placed in a more pre-eminent position.

John Mackinnon moved into the home in 1857 as the first

59 Ibid. page 35.

Earnscliffe—Daughter Mary's bench.

owner. There is recorded repeated mortgaging and Mackinnon died in 1866 heavily in debt. Another of McKay's sons-in-law, Thomas Keefer, bought Earnscliffe with its $6000 mortgage for $48.00. Keefer put the house up for auction in 1868 and it was sold for $7,500 to Thomas Reynolds, an Englishman involved in Ottawa's railways.

Reynolds returned to England in 1871 because of ill health and rented it to Sir John in 1871 for the winter.

Twelve years later the Macdonalds were able to buy the house for $10,000 from Thomas Reynolds's eldest son. At this time Sir John was sixty-seven years of age.

Before the Macdonalds moved in wife Agnes refurbished the house at a cost of $7000. She designed a new dining room and an office for the private secretary to Sir John, Joseph Pope, who had started work for him in 1882.

The splendid dining room which John A. used frequently for dinner parties still exists as does Pope's office. The dining table could sit up to twenty-four guests.

Earnscliffe, deck for Mary.

On an attached bench on the stair-well above the entrance to the dining room, the disabled daughter Mary, used to sit to watch guests going in to dinner. This is the only piece of furniture that still exists from the Macdonald era.

Sir John also had a special deck built at the west end of the house for his daughter to sit on in her wheelchair. The deck has long disappeared.

The house itself had been constructed of locally quarried limestone. It was designed in the Gothic Revival style with steeply pitched gables, ornamental bargeboards at the ends of the gables, clustered chimneys and mouldings crowning the windows.

There are a few descriptions of Earnscliffe written by eyewitnesses in Sir John's time: Lady Macdonald wrote about the house on New Year's Day 1871 when the Macdonalds had rented it for the winter.

My home is on a cliff, fringed with low trees, the windows in the rear overlook the river. When we came here, two months ago, the waters were broad and blue. Now they are all frozen and snow-covered. It is a stern picture now, all frosty, bound for winter.[60]

The next day, January 2, there was a reception at Earnscliffe and after the guests had gone she wrote:

All the fires blazing and crackling, the house in its best order, all the servants important and in a hurry and I in my best black velveteen gown, receiving New Year's visitors! The house was thronged from noon till dinner time, with men of all ages, sorts and styles. Some 130 in all—some merely shook hands or bowed, exchanged a few common-places about the weather, but the larger part lunched at a continually replenished table in the dining room and wished me and mine all the happiness of the New Year between mouthfuls of hot oyster soup or sips of sherry.[61]

A friend of John A. in his youth and a loyal political supporter, Eliza Grimason, was shown around the house in 1889 and related her experience to her friends. Mrs. Grimason had a Kingston tavern which was for years Macdonald's local election headquarters.

They do have a lovely place in their town, down there by the Rideau. The house has a lovely slate roof like they have in England and beauti-ful grounds, and everything in style, an' a man to wait on them. Lady Macdonald keeps her own cow and hens, and they make their own butter. They have two fine cows and six servants.[62]

Joseph Pope relates an incident at Earnscliffe but it reveals more of Sir John's personality than the residence.

Upon one occasion when Sir John was about to enter the grounds of

---

60 Louise Reynolds, *Agnes*, page 64.
61 Ibid., page 68.
62 Ibid., page 126.

Earnscliffe, Macdonald's Library 1891.

Earnscliffe, a reckless butcher boy driving down Sussex Street at a furious pace, charged full tilt into the side of his carriage and one of the shafts of the cart barely missed the head of the Prime Minister. The coachman alighted and wanted to haul the boy from the cart. "Let him alone! Pass on!" said Sir John, "it is merely the etiquette of his profession."[63]

It was at Earnscliffe that Macdonald developed a system to transact his government business. As Pope writes, "He was compelled to seclude himself many hours a day in his 'workshop,' as he called it at Earnscliffe."[64]

Much effort was spent by the Macdonalds on entertaining. Sir John tried to have every Conservative member of the House of Commons and the Senate at Earnscliffe for dinner twice during the parliamentary session.

---

63 Pope, page 9.
64 Ibid., page 630.

Earnscliffe, Macdonald's office, 1891.

After Sir John's death in 1891, Queen Victoria gave Lady Macdonald the title of Baroness Macdonald of Earnscliffe. Agnes decided to move to England with Mary and sold the house in 1900 for $15,000 together with the contents by auction. The large sale of furniture etc. which lasted three days included the bed in which Sir John had died.

The Baroness outlived her husband by thirty years and died in 1921.

The new owner of Earnscliffe who purchased it in 1900 was Dr. Charles Harriss. The Canadian Government could have bought it at that time for that low amount of $15,000. Mrs. Harriss made alterations to the dining room and Sir John's study was used as a music room by her husband.

After the death of Mrs. Harriss in 1924 her husband lived on at Earnscliffe until he died in 1930. At that time many other items of Sir John's were sold at auction and the house came on the market again.

According to Norman Reddaway, it was known at that time that the leaders of the Canadian Government of the day were considering the

Macdonald bust in the front hall at Earnscliffe.

idea of acquiring it as the Prime Minister's official residence or as the home of the leader of the Conservative Party.

Unfortunately, Conservative Prime Minister R. B. Bennett decided not to purchase it because of his sister's reluctance, who then kept house for him, to take on the large residence of Earnscliffe.

So R. B. Bennett remained at the Hotel Chateau Laurier and the United Kingdom Government purchased Earnscliffe in 1930 for $90,000. And thus, this heritage house, so important in Canadian history, became a no trespassing area for Canadians because it was now a diplomatic residence.

Possibly, too, R. B. Bennett felt the $90,000 was too much money for Canadian taxpayers when a depression had commenced in the United States and Canada.

In any event it was a grievous error for many reasons.

Since the home of the first president of the United States, George Washington, opened to the public in 1880, over eighty million people have visited it.

Imagine the uproar if the Queen of England, Elizabeth the Second, sold Windsor Castle or Buckingham Palace to Bill Gates of the United States.

There is a "Doors Open" program which has operated in Ottawa since 2002 that allows the public to visit historic and heritage buildings in that city for two days in June. Earnscliffe is included, but only every two years.

Sadly, today, the only evidence of Sir John A. Macdonald's presence inside Earnscliffe is a bust of him presented in 1930 by Prime Minister Bennett to mark the purchase of the house by the British Government.

As was mentioned on page 79 there is no original furniture except for the bench installed by Sir John for his daughter.

The first British High Commissioner who moved into Earnscliffe, Sir William Clark, divided up the attic floor into a number of bedrooms and increased the bathrooms from four to seven. The second occupant, Sir Francis Floyd, glassed in the terrace and in 1956 Sir Archibald Nye incorporated the terrace into an extension to the drawing room.

Earnscliffe was only declared a National Historic Site in 1960 and it is presumed there will be no more alterations.

A list of British High Commissioners shows a turnover of residents every two to six years.

Sir William Clark – 1930-1934
Sir Francis Floyd – 1938-1941
Sir Gerald Campbell – 1941-1946
Mr. Malcolm MacDonald—son of British Prime Minister
     Ramsey MacDonald – 1946-1952
Sir Alexander Clutterbuck – 1952-1956
Sir Archibald Nye – 1956-1961

Sir Saville Garner – 1961-1963
Viscount Amory – 1963-1968
Sir Henry Lintott – 1968-1970
Sir Colin Crowe – 1970-1974
Sir Peter Hayman – 1974-1978
Sir John Johnston – 1978-1981
Sir John Ford – 1981-1984
Lord Moran – 1984-1987
Sir Derek Day – 1987-1989
Sir Alan Urwick – 1989-1992
Mr. Brian Fall – 1992-1996
Mr. Nicholas Bayne – 1996-2000
Mr. Anthony Goodenough – 2000-2003
Sir Andrew Burns – 2003-2006
Mr. David Reddaway—son of Norman Reddaway, author of
    Earnscliffe, published in 1955 – 2007
Mr. Anthony Cary – 2007 to present

Mr. Cary's wife, Clare, graciously escorted the author and his wife on a tour of Earnscliffe in June of 2008.

Why is it important that Canada acquire Earnscliffe? Because the person who lived there was important.

Today Canada is in great need of dedication, love of country, political participation and a large heart. This was part and parcel of Sir John A. Macdonald.

Canadians should make a step towards demonstrating to ourselves that the past that created Canada is worthy of an effort by our government to purchase the home where Macdonald lived and died.

Expropriation and purchase of private to public homes is not unprecedented in Canada. Twenty-four Sussex Drive was expropriated in 1947. It took three years for the Canadian Supreme Court to rule on financial compensation and it was not until 1950 that the remodeled house became the official residence of Canada's Prime Ministers. The Right Honourable Louis St. Laurent moved there in 1951.

Likewise with "Stornaway," home of Canada's leader of the opposition. It was not until 1971 that the government took over that home as one of its official residences.

Another property of Harrington Lake was purchased by the Canadian government in 1951 and in 1959 became the official country residence for Prime Ministers.

These arrangements show that "where there is a will, there is a way," and Earnscliffe should be the next acquisition by Canada.

Hopefully, a new interest has emerged on the part of the Government of Canada. In 1999 a historic places initiative was conceived with three objectives:

"To foster greater appreciation of historic places.
To take action to conserve and maintain the historical integrity of historic places, and
To provide financial incentives that will make the preservation and rehabilitation of historic places more viable."

A "Canada's Historic Places" booklet gives further information including a government $24 million investment.

Another government booklet gives "Standards and Guidelines for the Conservation of Historic Places in Canada." It states among other things to "Make any intervention needed. . ."

These objectives could be applied to the acquisition of Earnscliffe. As Margaret MacMillan states, "The Department of Canadian Heritage exhorts Canadians to learn about Canada's history, culture and land. Heritage is our collective treasure, given to us to bequeath to our children."[65]

It would also give our first Prime Minister fuller recognition in Canada and would be a step forward in making everyone more aware of him. Earnscliffe is located on an aesthetically pleasing site, is placed in the capital city of Canada and is easy for citizens to find.

---

65 *Margaret MacMillan, The Uses and Abuses of History*, Penguin, Toronto, 2008, page 4.

Over 20,000 historic places have already been recognized in Canada and, "historic places capture the soul and spirit of our country."[66]

They not only attract our own citizens but also tourists from other countries.

There is already a recognition of the importance of Prime Ministers' homes. Laurier House, built in 1878, is a National Historic Site. It is located a few doors from Stadacona Hall on Laurier Avenue.

It commemorates Sir Wilfred Laurier who lived there from 1897 to 1919 and former Prime Minister William Lyon Mackenzie King who resided in the house from 1923 to 1950 when he died. The latter gave it to the "Government and People of Canada" and the Laurier House Act of 1951 passed by the House of Commons outlined how the house would be administered for its operation. It is now owned and operated by Parks Canada.

This author has visited Laurier House and found it lacking in important historical significance compared to Earnscliffe. This is borne out by the number of visitors.

Patrick Dare writing in the *Ottawa Citizen* on August 10, 2007 said that attendance at Laurier House was dwindling. "Despite a fascinating collection and modest admission charge, only 886 visitors entered the museum last month. Many assume it is an embassy and pass on by."

Bruno Schrumburger also of the *Ottawa Citizen* wrote "In the past decade, attendance has fallen from more than 10,000 visitors a year to fewer than 7,000."

On November 15, 2007, the *Vancouver Sun* reported the results of a survey by the polling firm Ipsos Reid.

Sir John who?
   The recent 2007 history survey among young Canadians shows that knowledge of Canada's political history isn't great, and has become worse over the last 10 years.
   Percentage that knew the year of Confederation: 26% (36% in 1997)

---

66 Brochure: *Canada's Historic Places.*

Plaque on private entrance to grounds of Earnscliffe.

Knew the name of Canada's first prime minister: 46% (54%)
Knew that Newfoundland was the last province to join Confedera-
tion: 38% (51%)
Knew that Louis Riel was hanged by the federal government in
1885: 27% (40%)

The acquisition of Earnscliffe would assist in remedying the lack of knowledge of our history. By including this Macdonald home as part of historic Ottawa, future generations could visit the place where Macdonald lived in the last nine years of his life, where he entertained politicians and dignitaries and where he conducted the business of being the first Prime Minister of Canada.

For many young Canadians, the only recollection they have of Sir John A. Macdonald is the reproduced picture of the Fathers of Confederation in Quebec with Macdonald as the tall figure in the centre.

Earnscliffe represents something that Canadians can share and take pride in. It is part of our roots and should have a Canadian flag, rather than a British flag, flying above it. It would thus mark the heritage home of Canada's greatest historical figure.

What makes our nation, in part, is our common history and our citizens' determination to continue to do good things together in the future. Earnscliffe is an essential image and legacy in our history, particularly of Confederation, and should be owned by Canada. In the words of American President Obama, "Yes, we can."

As part of the heritage conservation for Canadians that historic and stately home should be acquired by our government as a shrine in Canadian history. We would be doing this for future generations.

The House of Commons, as a first step, should pass a bill which would allow the government to approach British authorities with the request that Earnscliffe be resold to Canada. The "Standing Committee on Canadian Heritage," a House of Commons Parliamentary Committee should take the initiative on this.

With many Canadians emphasizing our country's history and heritage, this writer feels the ownership of Earnscliffe is important. It would be another ordinary miracle which fits the personality of our first Prime Minister who was the visionary of a Canada from coast to coast to coast.

It has been said by Frank Underhill that Canadians lack the capacity to be caught up in action for an idea.[67]

Let us prove that he is wrong and that in the national interest Earnscliffe should be made available to our young people in particular and all citizens in general. It is a symbol that will serve to further unite us as a nation.

---

67 Frank Underhill, *The Image of Confederation*, page 164.

CHAPTER EIGHT

Conclusion

"The teaching of history is important because knowledge of the past is prerequisite to political intelligence."[68]

—J. L. Granatstein

"History has shaped our values, our fears, our aspirations, our loves, and our hatreds. When we start to realize that, we begin to understand something of the power of the past."[69]

—Margaret MacMillan

Knowing the past is of inestimable benefit to all Canadians as we search for answers to many problems of modern life.

We must therefore raise an awareness of Canada's history in all its richness and complexity—particularly of Sir John A. Macdonald.

The story of Canada's first Prime Minister is one that adult citizens should know and share with young people.

A positive goal for our country is to create a unified national identity. This can be done by energetic teaching of Canada in schools about who we are as a nation and how much we have achieved. Our democracy requires citizens to be historians so that he or she can be more informed at election time. Canadians should have a Charter of Obligations as well as a Charter of Rights.

---

68 Granatstein, *Who Killed Canadian History?*, page 21.
69 M. MacMillan, *The Uses and Abuses of History*, page 9.

Part of this would be using federal and provincial funds for student travel to Ottawa to see our Parliament in action and to visit historic sites including Earnscliffe.

An annual legacy to Confederation is Canada Day on the first day of July. This day each year gives us pride as Canadians but in the many speeches and articles produced Sir John is seldom mentioned. It should be emphasized that as flawed and imperfect as he was he had the miraculous ability to challenge others to help create the golden possibility of a greater Canada.

It is conceivable that there should be a national holiday on January 11 which is his birthday. In 2002 Parliament passed a bill recognizing January 11 as Sir John A. Macdonald Day. Since then nothing has been done.

In 2015 it will be Sir John's 200th birthday. Let us hope there will be celebrations and education to mark the event.

In comparison to George Washington, Father of the United States, there is little physical Canadian evidence. Washington is commemorated by a 500 foot tall monument, a capital city, a state, and a university.

We, Canadians, are forgetting our history. It should be realized that Canada has a proud Confederation story which amounts to a coming of age moment.

"Not only do a large percentage of our people have a bad knowledge of our history, it's getting worse, particularly among young people," said Marc Chalifoux, executive director of the Dominion Institute, a charitable organization that promotes Canadian history as a way of building a more active citizenry.[70]

A survey released on January 10, 2009 by the Dominion Institute found that only 58 percent of Canadians could name our first Prime Minister. In 1997 former Prime Minister Jean Chrétien said,

It is unacceptable that our youth may know all about computers, but so little about their country. We must find ways for young Canadians to

---

70 *Vancouver Sun*, Oct. 16, 2008.

learn what they share, to know what we have done, and to gain pride in their nation's accomplishments. The Government of Canada will work with our government museum, other federal and provincial institutions and with voluntary groups to develop ways to increase Canadians' knowledge of what we have done together.[71]

It is clear that Canadians know very little about their past. Our history is a proud saga of nationhood and John A. Macdonald is an inspiring part of it.

From contemporary witnesses to recent historians, there is a lack of agreement on Macdonald's convictions, behaviour, ethics, and political policies. However, all of them recognize that he was the most influential person in the development of Canada.

Tommy Douglas, former N.D.P. leader stated, "Macdonald was an immigrant who made good and who made Canada in the process."

Lester Pearson, former Liberal Prime Minister, also praised him. "He was a skilled practitioner of the art of politics. I wish I had some of his skills."

All past and present historians agree that Macdonald's personality made Confederation possible. There is no question that Sir John had extraordinary negotiating skills despite personal defects. He was truly an ordinary miracle in the making of Confederation.

His enormous contribution to Canada is unrivalled in our history. Many other Canadian statesmen had a better education and were without the health and alcohol weaknesses that Macdonald had. In spite of these handicaps, he accomplished more than any of them.

"John A. Macdonald has no equal. His vision and guiding hand moulded this nation."[72]

---

71 Granatstein, page 157.
72 Bob Plamondon, *Blue Thunder*, page 23.

Bibliography

Adam, Mercer, *The life and career of the Right Honourable Sir John A. Macdonald.* Rose Publishing, Toronto, Ontario, 1891.

Ajzenstat, Janet, ed. *Canada's founding debates.* Stoddart Publishing, Toronto, Ontario, 1999.

Angus, Margaret. *John A. lived here.* Brown and Martin, Kingston, Ontario, 1984.

Axworthy, Tom. Article in *Hill Times*, July 21, 2008. Canada's politics and government newsweekly, Ottawa, Ontario.

Berton, Pierre, *Flames across the border.* McClelland and Stewart, Toronto, Ontario, 1981.

Berton, Pierre, *Historic headlines.* McClelland and Stewart, Toronto, Ontario, 1967.

Berton, Pierre, *The national dream.* McClelland and Stewart, Toronto, Ontario, 1970.

Biggar, E. B. *Anecdotal life of Sir John A. Macdonald.* John Lovell and Son, 1891.

Bliss, Michael. *Right honourable men.* Harper Collins, Toronto, Ontario, 1994.

Bliss, Michael. *Confederation: a new nationality.* Grolier Limited, Toronto, Ontario, 1981.

Bolotenko, George. *A future defined, Canada from 1849 to 1873.* National Archives of Canada, Ottawa, Ontario, 1992.

Bourrie, Mark. *Canada's parliament buildings.* Hounslow Press, Toronto, Ontario, 1996.

Brown, R. C., and Prang, M. E., editors. *Confederation to 1949.* Prentice-Hall, Scarborough, Ontario, 1966.

Brown, Craig, ed. *The illustrated history of Canada.* Key Porter Books Ltd., Toronto, Ontario, 1997.

Bumsted, J. M. *A history of the Canadian peoples*. Oxford University Press, Don Mills, Ontario, 2003.

Busby, Brian, ed. *Great Canadian speeches*. Arcturus Publishing, London, England, 2008.

Cameron, Stevie. *Ottawa inside out*. Key Porter Books, Toronto, Ontario, 1989.

Carless, J.M.S. *Canada, a story of challenge*. Macmillan, Toronto, Ontario, 1970.

Centennial Historical Booklets, Centennial Commission, Ottawa, Ontario, 1967.

Farr, D. L. M. *Great Britain and Confederation*.

MacNutt, W. S. *The Maritimes and Confederation*.

Hamelin, Jean. *First Years of Confederation*.

Roby, Yves. *The United States and Confederation*.

Swainson, D. *Ontario and Confederation*.

Waite, P. B. *The Charlottetown Conference*.

Morton, W. L. *The West and Confederation*.

Cornell, D. G. *The Great Coalition*.

Whitelaw, W. M. *The Quebec Conference*.

Bonenfant, J. C. *The French Canadians and the birth of Confederation*.

Cohoe, Margaret (compiler). *Sir John A. Macdonald 1815-1891*. Kingston Historical Society, Kingston, Ontario, 1991.

Collins, J. E. *Life and times of the Right Honourable Sir John A. Macdonald*. Rose Publishing, Toronto, Ontario, 1883.

Colombo, John. *Colombo's Canadian quotations*. Hurtig Publishers, Edmonton, Alberta, 1974.

Creighton, Donald. *John A. Macdonald*. University of Toronto Press, Toronto, Ontario, 1998.

Creighton, Donald. *The road to confederation*. Greenwood Press, Wesport, Connecticut, 1964.

Dictionary of Canadian Biography, Vol. 9 1861-1870. University of Toronto Press, Toronto, Ontario, 1976.

Donaldson, Gordon. *The prime ministers of Canada*. Doubleday Canada Limited, Toronto, Ontario, 1994.

Finkel, Alvin. *Winners and losers: Canadian national development, 1867-1900.* Athabaska University, Athabaska, Canada, 1986.

Finley, J. L., and Sprague, D. N. *Structure of Canadian history.* Prentice-Hall, Scarborough, Ontario, 1989.

Forsey, Eugene. *How Canadians govern themselves.* House of Commons, Public Interaction Office, Ottawa, Ontario, 1997.

Gillmor, Don, and Turgeon, Pierre. *Canada, a people's history, vol. one.* McClelland and Stewart, Toronto, Ontario, 2000.

Government of Canada, *Canada's historic places initiative.* Government Printing Office, Ottawa, Ontario, 2007.

Granatstein, J. L. *Who killed Canadian history?* Harper Collins, Toronto, Ontario, 2007.

Guillet, Edwin. *You'll never die, John A.!* Macmillan of Canada, Toronto, Ontario, 1907.

Gwyn, Richard. *John A. the man who made us.* Random House, Canada, 2007.

Habron, John D. *Century 1867-1967.* Stewart and Morrison, Vancouver, B.C., 1967.

Hammond, M. O. *Confederation and its leaders.* Warwick and Rutter, Toronto, Ontario, 1917.

Hancock, Pat. *The kids book of Canadian prime ministers.* Kids Can Press, Toronto, Ontario, 1998.

Hardy, W. G. *From sea to sea, 1850-1910.* Doubleday, Garden City, New York, 1960.

Hayes, Derek. *Historical atlas of Canada.* Douglas and McIntyre, University of Washington Press, Seattle, Washington, 2002.

Hird, Edward. *Battle for the soul of Canada.* Friesons Corporation, Altona, M. B., 2007.

Hitsman, J. MacKay, *The incredible war of 1812.* University of Toronto Press, Toronto, Ontario, 1965.

Hux, Allan. *My country, our history.* Pippon Publishing, Toronto, Ontario, 2002.

Jefferys, C. W. *The formative years, Canada 1812-1871.* The Ryerson Press, Toronto, Ontario, 1968.

Johnson, J. K., ed. *The letters of Sir John A. Macdonald*, Volume I and II. Queen's Printer, Ottawa, Ontario, 1968.

Kilbourne, William. *The making of the nation.* The Canadian Centennial Publishing Co., Ltd. Toronto, Ontario, 1965.

Leacock, Stephen. *Canada the foundations of its future.* Privately printed, Montreal, Canada, 1941.

Lower, J.A. *Canada, an outline history.* McGraw-Hill Ryerson, Toronto, Ontario, 1973.

MacMillan, Margaret. *The uses and abuses of history.* Penguin Group, Toronto, Ontario, 2008.

Macskimming, Roy. *Macdonald.* Thomas Allen, Toronto, Ontario, 2007.

Manson, Ainslie. *Baboo, the story of Sir John A. Macdonald's daughter.* Douglas and McIntyre, Toronto, Ontario, 1998.

Martin, Ged. *Britain and the origins of Canadian confederation 1837-67.* UBC Press, Vancouver, B.C., 1995.

Martin, Ged, ed. *The causes of Canadian confederation.* Acadiensis Press, Fredericton, New Brunswick, 1990.

Masters, D. C. *Reciprocity 1846-1911.* Canadian Historical Association, Ottawa, Ontario, 1983.

Mclennan, Rob, *Ottawa, the unknown city.* Arsenal Pulp Press, Vancouver, BC, 2008.

McTeer, Maureen. *Residences, homes of Canada's leaders.* Prentice-Hall, Scarborough, Ontario, 1982.

Mika, Nick, and Mika, Helma. *Kingston, a historic city.* Mika Publishing, Kingston, Ontario, 1987.

Moore, Christopher. *1867, How the fathers made a deal.* McClelland and Stewart, Toronto, Ontario, 1997.

Morton, Desmond. *A short history of Canada.* McClelland and Stewart, Toronto, Ontario, *1994.*

Morton, W. L. *The critical years, 1857-1873.* McClelland and Stewart, Toronto, Ontario, 1964.

National Archives of Canada. *Treasures of the national archives of Canada.* University of Toronto Press, Toronto, Ontario, 1992.

Neidhardt, W. S. *Fenianism in North America*. The Pennsylvania State University Press, University Park, Pennsylvania, 1975.

Newman, Lena. *The John A. Macdonald album*. Tundra Books, Montreal, Quebec, 1974.

Newman, Peter C. *Renegade in power: the Diefenbaker years*. McClelland and Stewart, Toronto, Ontario, 1973.

Ondaatje, Christopher. *The prime ministers of Canada*. Pagurian Press, Toronto, Ontario, 1985.

Parkin, George R. *Sir John A. Macdonald*. Morang and Company, Toronto, Ontario, 1903.

Phenix, Patricia. *Private demons, the tragic personal life of John A. Macdonald*. McClelland and Stewart, Toronto, Ontario, 2006.

Plamonden, Bob. *Blue thunder, the truth about Conservatives from Macdonald to Harper*. Key Porter Books Limited, Toronto, Ontario, 2009.

Pope, Joseph. *Memoirs of the Right Honourable Sir John Alexander Macdonald*. Oxford University Press, Canada, 1930.

Reddaway, Norman. *Earnscliffe*. Commonwealth Relations Office, London, 1955.

Reynolds, Louise. *Agnes, the biography of Lady Macdonald*. Carleton University Press, Ottawa, Ontario, 1990.

Robertson, Heather. *More than a rose, Prime Ministers, wives and other women*. McClelland-Banton, Inc., Toronto, Ontario, 1991.

Senior, Hereward. *The last invasion of Canada 1866-1870*. Dundurn Press, Toronto, Ontario, 1991.

Shelton, George. *British Columbia and Confederation*. Morriss Printing, Victoria, B.C., 1967.

Smith, Cynthia, and McLeod, Jack, editors. *Sir John A. an anecdotal life of John A. Macdonald*. Oxford University Press, Toronto, Ontario, 1989.

Spalding-Smith, F., and Humphreys, B. *Legacy in stone—the Rideau corridor*. The Boston Mills press, Toronto, Canada, 1999.

Sprague, Douglas. *Post Confederation Canada: the structure of Canadian history since 1867*. Prentice-Hall, Scarborough, Ontario, 1990.

Steinor, Rosalyn, ed. *Colonies: Canada to 1867*. McGraw-Hill Ryerson, Toronto, Ontario, 1992.

Stewart, Douglas, and Wilson, Ian. *Heritage Kingston*. Queens University, Kingston, Ontario, 1973.

Swainson, Donald. *Macdonald of Kingston*. Thomas Nelson and Sons, Don Mills, Ontario, 1979.

Swainson, Donald. *Sir John A. Macdonald, the man and the politician*. Quarry Press, Kingston, Ontario, 1989.

Talman, James J. *Basic documents in Canadian history*. Van Nostrand Co., Toronto, Ontario, 1966.

Underhill, Frank. *The Image of Confederation*. CBC Publications, Toronto, Ontario, 1964.

Waite, P. B. *Macdonald, his life and world*. McGraw-Hill Ryerson, Toronto, Ontario, 1975.

Waite, Peter. *Canada 1874-1896*. McClelland and Stewart, Toronto, Ontario, 1971.

Waite, Peter. *The life and times of Confederation 1864-1867*. Robin Brass Studio, Toronto, Ontario, 2001.

Wolf, Jim. *Royal City 1888-1960*. Heritage House Publishing, Surrey, B.C., 2005.

Wood, Gordon. *The purpose of the past*. Penguin Press, New York, 2008.

Woodcock, George, *The Canadians*. Fitzhenry and Whiteside, Don Mills, Ontario, 1979.

Woodland, Alan. *Eminent guests*. Corporation of the City of New Westminster, British Columbia, Canada, 2003.

Index